Presented to

....

By

....

On the Occasion of

....

Date

....

100 Devotions

from Charles Spurgeon

ENCOURAGEMENT

FOR TROUBLING TIMES

CHARLES SPURGEON

BARBOUR
PUBLISHING

Editorial assistance by Lee Warren

ISBN 979-8-89151-233-7

All scripture quotations are taken from the King James Version of the Bible.

Cover design by Greg Jackson, Thinkpen Design

Published by Barbour Publishing, Inc., 1810 Barbour Drive, Uhrichsville, Ohio 44683, www.barbourbooks.com

Our mission is to inspire the world with the life-changing message of the Bible.

Printed in China.

NEED HOPE IN A WORLD GONE MAD?

HERE IS DEEP YET ACCESSIBLE ENCOURAGEMENT FROM ONE OF HISTORY'S GREATEST PREACHERS.

Charles Spurgeon, "the Prince of Preachers," is well remembered and remarkably readable some 130 years after his death. This devotional, compiled from his decades of weekly sermons, is designed to encourage Christian men in an increasingly troubled world—assuring you that in uncertain times, you have an unchanging God.

On the pages to follow you'll find 100 thoughtful entries with titles such as

- Whatever Else Changes, God Does Not
- Let Not Your Heart Be Troubled
- Be Thankful for Trouble
- Change Should Be Expected
- The Approachable Jesus

Entries have been lightly edited for spelling, capitalization, and punctuation. While some text has been removed for reasons of length, no changes have been made to Spurgeon's arguments or thought process. We have chosen not to use ellipses to indicate the removal of words so as not to disrupt the flow of your reading. Each meditation is accompanied by a brief description of its source.

Encouragement for Troubling Times is a powerful, necessary book for our times. Read on to find the strength you need for difficult days.

WHATEVER ELSE CHANGES, GOD DOES NOT

For I am the Lord, I change not;
therefore ye sons of Jacob are not consumed.

Malachi 3:6

Whatever the attributes of God were of old, that they are now.

Was He powerful? Was He the mighty God when He spake the world out of the womb of non-existence? Was He the Omnipotent when He piled the mountains and scooped out the hollow places for the rolling deep? Yes, He was powerful then and His arm is unpalsied now. He is the same giant in His might.

Was He wise when He constituted this mighty globe, when He laid the foundations of the universe? Had He wisdom when He planned the way of our salvation, and when from all eternity He marked out His awful plans? Yes, and He is wise now. He is not less skillful, He has not less knowledge. His eye which sees all things is undimmed, His ear which hears all the cries, sighs, sobs, and groans of His people, is not rendered heavy by the years which He has heard their prayers.

He is unchanged in His wisdom. He knows as much now

as ever, neither more nor less. He has the same consummate skill and the same infinite forecastings.

He is unchanged in His truth. He has promised, and He brings it to pass. He has said it, and it shall be done. He varies not in the goodness and generosity and benevolence of His nature.

And blessed be His dear name, He is unchanged in His love. When He first wrote the covenant, how full His heart was with affection to His people. He knew that His Son must die to ratify the articles of that agreement. He knew right well that He must rend His best beloved from His bowels and send Him down to earth to bleed and die.

He did not hesitate to sign that mighty covenant, nor did He shun its fulfillment. He loves as much now as He did then, and when suns shall cease to shine, and moons to show their feeble light, He still shall love on forever and forever. Take any one attribute of God and I will write *semper idem* on it ("always the same"). Take any one thing you can say of God now and it may be said not only in the dark past, but in the bright future—it shall always remain the same, "I am JEHOVAH, I change not."

"THE IMMUTABILITY OF GOD,"
NEW PARK STREET PULPIT, NO. 1 (1855)

BE THANKFUL FOR TROUBLE

Thy wrath lieth hard upon me, and thou hast afflicted me with all thy waves. Selah.

PSALM 88:7

Severe trouble in a true believer has the effect of loosening the roots of his soul earthward and tightening the anchor-hold of his heart heavenward. How can he love the world which has become so drear to him? Why should he seek after grapes so bitter to his taste? Should he not now ask for the wings of a dove, that he may fly away to his own dear country and be at rest forever?

Every mariner on the sea of life knows that when the soft zephyrs blow, men tempt the open sea with outspread sails. But when the black tempest comes howling from its den, they hurry with all speed to the haven. Afflictions clip our wings with regard to earthly things so that we may not fly away from our dear Master's hand, but sit there and sing to Him. But the same afflictions make our wings grow with regard to heavenly things—we are feathered like eagles, we catch the soaring spirit, a thorn is in our nest, and we spread our pinions toward the sun.

Affliction frequently opens truths to us and opens us to the truth—I know not which of these two is the more difficult. Experience unlocks truths which else were closed against us. Many passages of scripture will never be made clear by the commentator—they must be expounded by experience.

I have heard that you see stars in a well when none are visible above ground, and I am sure you can discern many a starry truth when you are down in the deeps of trouble which would not be visible to you elsewhere.

Affliction, as it were, plows us and sub-soils us, and opens up our hearts so that into our innermost nature the truth penetrates and soaks like rain into plowed land. Blessed is that man who receives the truth of God into his inmost self—he shall never lose it, but it shall be the life of his spirit.

Affliction, when sanctified by the Holy Spirit, brings much glory to God out of Christians through their experience of the Lord's faithfulness to them.

"For the Troubled,"
Metropolitan Tabernacle Pulpit, No. 1090 (1873)

JUST AS SAFE

A bruised reed shall he not break, and smoking flax shall he not quench, till he send forth judgment unto victory.

MATTHEW 12:20

These saints of God who are called bruised reeds and smoking flax are just as safe as those who are mighty for their Master, and great in strength, for several reasons. First of all, the little saint is just as much God's elect as the great saint. When God chose His people, He chose them all at once, and altogether; and He elected one just as much as the other. If I choose a certain number of things, one may be less than the rest, but one is as much chosen as the other; and so Mrs. Fearing and Miss Despondency are just as much elected as Great-Heart, or Old Father Honest.

Again, the little ones are redeemed equally with the great ones! The feeble saints cost Christ as much suffering as the strong ones; the tiniest child of God could not have been purchased with less than Jesus' precious blood; and the greatest child of God did not cost Him more. Paul did not cost any more than Benjamin—I am sure he did not—for I read in the Bible that "there is no difference."

Besides, when of old they came to pay their redemption money, every person brought a shekel. The poor shall bring no less, and the rich shall bring no more than just a shekel. The same price was paid for the one as the other. Now then, little child of God, take that thought to thy soul. You see some men very prominent in Christ's cause—and it is very good that they should be—but they did not cost Jesus a farthing more than you did; He paid the same price for you that He paid for them.

Recollect again, you are just as much a child of God as the greatest saint. Some of you have five or six children. There is one child of yours, perhaps, who is very tall and handsome, and has, moreover, gifts of mind; and you have another child who is the smallest of the family, perhaps has but little intellect and understanding. But which is the most your child? "The most!" you say. "Both alike are my children, certainly, one as much as the other." And so, dear friends, you are as much the children of God as those who have grown to the stature of men in Christ Jesus.

"SWEET COMFORT FOR FEEBLE SAINTS,"
NEW PARK STREET PULPIT, NO. 6 (1855)

WE HAVE CONSOLATION

For as the sufferings of Christ abound in us,
so our consolation also aboundeth by Christ.

2 CORINTHIANS 1:5

Seek ye rest from your distresses, ye children of woe and sorrow? This is the place where ye may lighten your burden and lose your cares. Oh, son of affliction and misery, wouldst thou forget for a time thy pains and griefs? This is the Bethesda, the house of mercy; this is the place where God designs to cheer thee, and to make thy distresses stay their never-ceasing course; this is the spot where His children love to be found, because here they find consolation in the midst of tribulation, joy in their sorrows, and comfort in their afflictions.

Even worldly men admit that there is something extremely comforting in the sacred scriptures, and in our holy religion; I have even heard it said of some, that after they had, by their logic, as they thought, annihilated Christianity and proved it to be untrue, they acknowledged that they had spoiled an excellently comforting delusion, and that they could almost sit down and weep to think it was not a reality.

Ay, my friends, if it were not true, ye might weep. If the

Bible were not the truth of God—if we could not meet together around His mercy seat, then ye might put your hands upon your loins and walk about as if ye were in travail.

If ye had not something in the world beside your reason, beside the fleeting joys of earth—if ye had not something which God had given to you, some hope beyond the sky, some refuge that should be more than terrestrial, some deliverance which should be more than earthly, then ye might weep. Ah! Weep your heart out at your eyes, and let your whole bodies waste away in one perpetual tear. Ye might ask the clouds to rest on your head, the rivers to roll down in streams from both your eyes, for your grief would "have need of all the watery things that nature could produce." But, blessed be God, we have consolation, we have joy in the Holy Ghost. We find it nowhere else.

"Consolation Proportionate to Spiritual Sufferings,"
New Park Street Pulpit, No. 13 (1855)

FAITH WILL DELIVER YOU

Give ye them to eat.

MARK 6:37

Surely it ought not to be difficult for a child to believe his father; it should not therefore be difficult for us to trust in our God today, and so to lift our spirits out of the tumult of their doubts.

Somebody will say, "Well, I can understand that faith is a practical way of getting out of trouble, but I cannot understand how we are to have faith." Well, in this the Savior helps us. You remember what He said when the people were hungering: "Give ye them to eat." "Ah," they said, "there are so many; how can we feed them?" The Master began by saying, "How many loaves have ye?" That is just what He says here. He says, "It is faith that will get you out of trouble; but how much faith have you?" He answers for them, "Ye believe in God." I must do the same by you.

Faith is that which will deliver you. You say, "Where am I to get it?" Well, you have some already, have you not? You have five barley loaves and a few small fishes. You are unbelieving creatures, but you have some measure of faith. You believe that there is a God. "Ay," you say. You believe He is unchangeable, you believe that He is full of love, good and kind, and true and faithful. Now, really that is a great deal to begin with.

You believe in God; the most of us believe in a great deal more than that. We not only believe in a God, and in the excellence of His character, but we believe that He has a chosen people, that He has made with them a covenant, ordered in all things and sure, that the promises of His covenant will be fulfilled, that He never puts away His people; we believe that all things work together for good to them that love God; we believe that the blood of Jesus Christ, His Son, cleanseth us from all sin; we believe that the Holy Ghost is given to dwell in His people. Now this is a great deal, a solid fulcrum upon which to place the lever.

"Let Not Your Hearts Be Troubled,"
Metropolitan Tabernacle Pulpit, No. 730 (1867)

HELP IN GOD

He will be very gracious unto thee at the voice of thy cry; when he shall hear it, he will answer thee.

ISAIAH 30:19

You are depressed at this time by heavy grief. Things have gone amiss with you: You do not prosper in business, or you are sickening in body, or a dear one lies at home pining away. We do not wonder that you feel exceedingly burdened in spirit. At the same time you are ill at ease as to your own state; the iron is entering into your soul. While passing through this thick darkness, you will be strongly tempted to think hardly of God and to blame Him for the troubles which now surround you; yet this will only make matters worse and increase your sin and your sorrow.

Peradventure also you will be ready to despair and say, "There is no hope, I am taken as in a net, and there is no escape for me," though if you knew all you would chase away despair as your greatest enemy. Possibly you will be ready to try some wrong method by way of helping yourself out of present straits.

Satan will suggest to you dishonest, impure, or reckless courses which hold out some shadow of relief. This is your danger at this time, and in pity to you the Lord bids us assure you that there is a far wiser course open to you; namely, to turn to Him, for He will be very gracious unto you at the voice of your cry, and when He hears it He will answer you.

There is help in God for your present trial, whatever form it assumes. Infinite wisdom understands it, and infinite power can help you through it. God can remove from you that which you are suffering, or He can prevent the occurrence of that which you dread; or if in His divine wisdom He shall see fit to lay the rod upon you, He can enable you to bear it, and make it to turn to your everlasting good.

Be well assured that He doth not afflict willingly, nor grieve the children of men out of any delight in their sorrows. He pities those who are afflicted, for He is very tender and full of compassion, and ever swift to succor the suffering.

"Encouragement to Trust and Pray,"
Metropolitan Tabernacle Pulpit, No. 1419 (1878)

GOD IS FOR YOU

What shall we then say to these things?
If God be for us, who can be against us?

ROMANS 8:31

Nothing good in this world can be effected without difficulty. The biggest diamonds lie under heavy stones which sluggards cannot turn over. That which is easy to do is hardly worth doing. In the face of difficulty the man of ardent, persevering spirit braces up his nerves, sharpens his wits, and brings all his powers into play to achieve an object that will reward his efforts. Have you great difficulties, dear friend? You are not the first worker for God who has had difficulties to encounter.

Let us go back to Moses; he was to bring Israel out of Egypt, but his path did not appear very plain. He must go before Pharaoh and issue God's command. Pharaoh looked him through when he said, "Let my people go." The haughty monarch was greatly surprised to hear anybody, especially a Hebrew, talk like that; and so he bade him begone. But Moses returns with, "Thus saith the Lord, Let my people go"; and his courage was not even then crowned with immediate success.

There must be plague upon plague, plague upon plague, till

at last proud Pharaoh's heart was broken. The Israelites were saved from the hand of him that hated them, and Egypt was glad when they departed. This, however, was but the beginning of the mission of Moses. His was a life of difficulty—the meekest man, but the most provoked; and until he got to the top of Pisgah, and his gracious Master kissed away his soul, the prophet of Horeb had never done with difficulties.

Any good thing, I say, especially any good thing done for God, must be surrounded with difficulties and resisted by adversaries. Look at Nehemiah and Ezra and Zerubbabel, and those that built Jerusalem the second time. These good men wrought zealously, but Sanballat and Tobiah were jeering and jesting and trying to throw down the wall. If you build a city without difficulty, it is not Jerusalem. Be sure of that. As soon as ever you begin working for God you will find a great power working against you. If you encounter opposition, take it as a good sign.

"Cheer Up, My Comrades!"
Metropolitan Tabernacle Pulpit, No. 1513 (1880)

AWAY WITH ANXIETIES

Casting all your care upon him; for he careth for you.

1 Peter 5:7

Each Christian will in his time have personal troubles of a higher order; namely, spiritual cares. He is begotten again unto a lively hope, but he fears that his faith will yet die. He hopes he has some spark of spiritual joy, but there are dark and dreary nights which lower over him, and he fears that his lamp will die out in darkness. As yet he has been victorious, but he trembles lest he should one day fall by the hand of the enemy.

Beloved, I beseech thee; cast this care upon God, for He careth for you. "I am persuaded that he that hath begun a good work in you will carry it on and perfect it unto the day of Christ." He hath said, "I will never leave thee, nor forsake thee." "The mountains shall depart, and the hills be removed; but my kindness shall not depart from thee, neither shall the covenant of my peace be removed, saith the Lord that hath mercy on thee." "When thou passest through the waters, I will be with thee; and through the rivers, they shall not overflow thee: when thou walkest through the fire, thou shalt not be burned; neither shall the flame kindle upon thee." "No good thing will I withhold from them that walk uprightly." "I give unto my sheep eternal life, and they shall never perish, neither shall any man pluck them out of my hand."

Away then with dark suspicions and anxieties! Is it care about past sin? "The blood of Jesus Christ, God's dear Son, cleanseth us from all sin." Is it present temptation? "There hath no temptation happened to you but such as is common to men: but God who is faithful, who will not suffer you to be tempted above that ye are able; but will with the temptation also make a way to escape, that ye may be able to bear it." Is it future peril? O leave thou that with Him, for neither "things present, nor things to come, nor height, nor depth, nor any other creature, shall be able to separate us from the love of God, which is in Christ Jesus our Lord."

"A Cure for Care,"
Metropolitan Tabernacle Pulpit, No. 428 (1862)

THE APPROACHABLE JESUS

And he said unto them, Why are ye troubled?
and why do thoughts arise in your hearts?

LUKE 24:38

Jesus Christ came into the world to save sinners. If He does not save sinners, then He came into this world to mock us. He came into this world for nothing, and if you, being a sinner, will come to Christ and Christ rejects you, He has forgotten His commission, He has belied His character. He must give up His name, for He is no longer Jesus if He does not save sinners that come to Him; ay, and if He does not save sinners that do not come to Him too, for He has come to seek and to save—both to seek and to save—that which was lost.

"But," says yet another, "I cannot think that the Lord Jesus Christ would take any notice of me." Oh, that I could nail your wretched, miserable thoughts of my great Lord up on His cross! "Oh, but I am nobody, sir." Christ died for nobodies. "But I am poor." "The poor have the gospel preached to them."

"But I am altogether obscure and unknown." Oh, no, you are not. The Lord Jesus knows all about you! Even the hairs of your head are all numbered. Do not suppose that if you were rich, Christ would think any more of you than He does now. You know how it is among men—if a man wears a good coat and a diamond ring, people give him a seat as soon as he comes into the aisle.

Ay, but that is not the spirit of Jesus Christ! He delighted to associate with the poorest of the poor.

Therefore, do not tell me that He will not condescend to look at you. My Lord would leave off listening to the songs of angels to hear a poor sinner cry. If it were some grand review day in heaven, when helmed cherubim and mailed seraphim marched before His august eye, He would leave the camp of angels to come and listen to a beggar's prayer. For remember, He is a man as truly as He is God, and everything that is human touches that true heart of His that was pierced for men.

"Christ the Cure for Troubled Hearts,"
Metropolitan Tabernacle Pulpit, No. 2408 (1887)

A WELL-SPRING OF COMFORT

For whatsoever things were written aforetime were written for our learning, that we through patience and comfort of the scriptures might have hope.

Romans 15:4

When you read the promise, and it is applied with power to you; when you read the precept, and it works with force upon your conscience; when you read any part of God's Word, and it gives life to your spirit—then it is that you get the comfort of it.

I have heard of persons reading so many chapters a day, and getting through the Bible in a year—a very admirable habit, no doubt. But it may be performed so mechanically that no good whatever may come of it. You want to pray earnestly over the Word, that it may quicken you, or otherwise it will not be a comfort to you. Let us think of what our comfort is in the time of affliction from our soul's being quickened by the Word. Comfort comes thus; God's Word has in past days quickened us. It has been a word of life from the dead.

In our affliction, we therefore remember how God has brought us out of spiritual death and made us alive, and this cheers us. If you can say, "Whatever pain I suffer, whatever grief I endure, yet I am a living child of God," then you have a well-spring of comfort. It is better to be the most afflicted child of God than to be the gayest worldling. Better to be God's dog than the devil's darling. Child of God, comfort yourself with this: If God has not given me a soft bed, nor left me a whole skin, yet He has quickened me by His Word; and this is a choice favor. Thus our first quickening from spiritual death is a sunny memory.

After we are made alive we need to be quickened in duty, to be quickened in joy, to be quickened in every holy exercise; and we are happy if the Word has given us this repeated quickening. If, in looking back, dear friend, you can say, "Thy Word hath quickened me; I have had much joy in hearing Thy Word; I have been made full of energy through Thy Word; I have been made to run in the way of Thy commandments through Thy Word"; all this will be a great comfort to you.

"My Comfort in Affliction,"
Metropolitan Tabernacle Pulpit, No. 1872 (1881)

A SHARP CHISEL

That I may know him, and the power of his resurrection, and the fellowship of his sufferings, being made conformable unto his death.

PHILIPPIANS 3:10

Beloved, ye remember that it is written that we "must bear the image of the heavenly"; namely, the image of Christ. As He was in this world, even so must we be. We must have fellowship with Him in His sufferings, that we may be conformable unto His death. Hast thou never thought that none can be like the Man of Sorrow unless they have sorrows too? How can you be like unto Him who sweat as it were great drops of blood, if you do not sometimes say, "My soul is exceeding sorrowful, even unto death"?

Think not, O well beloved, that thou canst be like the thorn-crowned head and yet never feel the thorn. Canst thou be like thy dying Lord, and yet be uncrucified? Must thy hand be without a nail, and thy foot without a wound? Canst thou be like Him, unless like Him thou art compelled to say, "My God, my God, why hast thou forsaken me?" God is chiseling you—you are but a rough block—He is making you into the image of Christ; and that sharp chisel is taking away much which prevents your being like Him. Must He who is our head be marred in His visage by reason of grief, and must we forever rejoice and sing? It cannot be.

The heirs of salvation, I know from his word,
Through much tribulation must follow their Lord.

Sweet is the affliction which gives us fellowship with Christ. Blessed is the plow that plows deep furrows, if the furrows be like His. Blessed is the mouth that spits upon us, if the spittle be from the same cause as that which defiled His face. Blessed are the nails and thorns and vinegar and spear, if they but make us somewhat like to Him, in whose glory we shall be partakers when we shall see Him as He is.

This is a matter which all cannot understand, for it is a path which no unhallowed foot hath trodden, and no careless eye hath so much as seen it. But the true believer can rejoice therein, for He has had fellowship with Christ in His sufferings.

"The Sweet Uses of Adversity,"
New Park Street Pulpit, No. 283 (1859)

NEEDLESS FEARS

Who art thou, that. . .hast feared continually every day because of the fury of the oppressor, as if he were ready to destroy? and where is the fury of the oppressor?

ISAIAH 51:12–13

Objects often influence us out of proportion to their value because of their nearness. For instance, the moon is a very small insignificant body compared with the sun, yet it has far more influence over the tides and many other matters in the world than the sun has simply because it is so much nearer to the earth than the sun is.

The life that is to come is infinitely more important than the life that now is, and I hope that in our inmost hearts, we reckon that the things that are seen and temporal are mere trifles compared with the things which are not seen and eternal; yet it often happens that the less important matters have a greater influence over us than those which are far more important, simply because the things of earth are so much nearer to us.

Heaven is infinitely more to be desired than any joy of earth, yet it seems far off, and hence these fleeting joys may give us greater present comfort. The wrath of God is far more to be dreaded than the anger of man, yet sometimes a frown or a rebuke from a fellow creature will have more effect upon our minds than the thought of the anger of God. This is because the one appears to be remote, while, being in this body, we are so near to the other.

Now, beloved, it will sometimes happen that a matter which is scarcely worthy of the thought of an immortal spirit, will fret and worry us from day to day. There is some oppressor, as the text puts it, whom we dread and fear continually; yet we forget the almighty God who is on our side, who is stronger than all the oppressors who have ever lived, and who has all people and all things under His control. The reason why we act thus is because we think of God as if He were far off, while we can see the oppressor with our eyes, and we can hear with our ears his threatening words.

I want at this time to be the means in the hands of God of turning the thoughts of His people away from the distress of the present to the joy and comfort which, though more remote, ought to still be more powerful over the mind and heart because of the real intrinsic greatness.

"Needless Fears,"
Metropolitan Tabernacle Pulpit, No. 3098 (1874)

DANCING HEARTS

The days of our years are threescore years and ten; and if by reason of strength they be fourscore years, yet is their strength labour and sorrow; for it is soon cut off, and we fly away.

PSALM 90:10

May the Lord open your eyes to see what you will be in Him. Ah, what will you be in Christ? In a very little while we shall be with Him. Many of our members have gone home to Jesus, and one very earnest brother, very diligent in working for the Master—a young man of whom we expected much, has been swept away by the receding tide while bathing in the sea, but He has gone to His rest, I doubt not. Older friends have also ascended to God just lately, rejoicing to enter into the joy of the Lord. Between now and next month's communion some of us will, probably, have departed to the Father.

Let our eyes be opened to behold by faith the glory soon to be revealed. It may almost make you laugh for joy to think of your head wearing a crown—that poor head of yours. These poor aching knees and weary feet, there will be no more toil for them. That poor scantily furnished room, and hard fare, and narrow means, and weary labor will all be exchanged for mansions of rest, bread of bliss, and new wine of delight.

You know each pavement stone between here and your house, for you come so often to the Tabernacle; but you will be walking the streets of gold before long to the eternal temple above. Instead of noisy streets you will traverse paths of rest, amid the songs of seraphs and the psalms of the redeemed; and that, perhaps, within a month. Yes, in less than it takes the moon to fill her horns you shall be where the Lord God and the Lamb are the eternal light.

Certain of us are nearer heaven than we think. Let our hearts dance for joy at the bare thought of such speedy felicity. Let us go on our way blessing and magnifying Him who has opened our eyes to see the glory which He has prepared for them that love Him, which shall be ours ere long.

"Eyes Opened,"
Metropolitan Tabernacle Pulpit, No. 1461B (1879)

THE UNSEEN

While we look not at the things which are seen, but at the things which are not seen: for the things which are seen are temporal; but the things which are not seen are eternal.

2 CORINTHIANS 4:18

You are in despondency about temporal affairs. What is the reason why you are in trouble? "Because," say you, "I never was in such a condition before in my life. Wave upon wave of trouble comes upon me. I have lost one friend and then another. It seems as if business had altogether run away from me. Once I had a flood-tide, and now it is an ebb, and my poor ship grates upon the gravel, and I find she has not water enough to float her—what will become of me? And, oh! Sir, my enemies have conspired against me in every way to cut me up and destroy me; opposition upon opposition threatens me. My shop must be closed; bankruptcy stares me in the face, and I know not what is to become of me."

You are looking at your trouble, not at the God who sent your trouble; you are looking at yourselves, not at the God who dwells within you, and who has promised to sustain you. He that is nearest to the kingdom of heaven would have cause to droop and die if he had nothing to look at but that which eye can see and ear can hear. What wonder then if thou art disconsolate, when thou hast begun to look at the things which always must be enemies to faith?

But I would remind you that you have forgotten to look to Christ since you have been in this trouble. I will not suppose that you have neglected prayer or have left your Bible unread; but still, have you had any of those sweet thoughts of Christ which once you had? Have you been able to take all your troubles to Him and say, "Lord, Thou knowest all things; I trust all in Thy hands?"

Let me ask you—have you considered that Christ is omnipotent and therefore able to deliver you; that He is faithful, and must deliver you, because He has promised to do so? Have you not kept your eye on His rod, and not on His hand? Oh, recollect that you can never find joy and peace while you are looking at the things that are seen.

"Mr. Fearing Comforted,"
New Park Street Pulpit, No. 246 (1859)

TAKE COURAGE

There remaineth therefore a rest to the people of God.

HEBREWS 4:9

We look from earthly mountains and we see, but we do not possess. That mansion yonder is not ours; that crystal abeam belongs not to us; those widespread lawns are beautiful, but they are not in our possession. But on the hilltops of heaven, all that we are we shall possess. We shall possess the streets of gold, the harps of harmony, the palms of victory, the shouts of angels, the songs of cherubim, the joy of the divine Trinity, and the song of God as He rears in His love and rejoices over us with singing—nay, God the Eternal One Himself shall be ours, and ours forever and forever.

What better encouragement can I give to you poor tired, wearied, and all but despairing Christians? Take courage. The last six days have tired you very much. Put away your trials today; you have had enough to cast you down, but is not the reflection of today enough to lift you up? Oh! Remember the summit will repay you for the toil in climbing it. Though rough may be the road, it is but short at the longest—and the rest, the rest, will make amends. O man! Men will suffer more to get rich than you do to be found in Christ. Go on, go on; stand fast in the Lord, my dearly beloved, and having done all, still stand.

Would that some here who have never tried to climb that mountain would remember that if they climb it not now, they will have to descend forever! If now they turn not their faces to the steep ascent and go up it like men, they must fall eternally. Good God, what a fall! On what slippery places do they stand! I see them reeling even now! What a desperate dash was that! They fall, they fall, on through darkness, through blackest darkness, black as death and hell; on, on they fall, for the pit is bottomless! No rest shall they ever reach, down, down descending from the lower depths to the lowest depths, from hell to hell's profounder deep, from eternity of woe, on, on, on to woe trebled, multiplied sevenfold!

May God grant that we, having faith in Christ, may tread the blood-marked way, and enter into "the rest which remaineth for the people of God!"

"Climbing the Mountain,"
Metropolitan Tabernacle Pulpit, No. 396 (1861)

THE RIGHT KIND OF FEAR

Happy is the man that feareth alway.

Proverbs 28:14

But did not John say that "fear hath torment"? Then how can he be happy who has fear, and especially he who has it always? Did not John also say that "perfect love casteth out fear"? How is it then, that he is happy in whom love is not made perfect, if so be that the fear which John meant is left in it? Dear friends, the explanation is that the word *fear* is used in different senses, and both Solomon and John are right; neither is there any conflict between their two statements.

There is a fear which perfect love casts out because it has torment. That is the slavish fear which trembles before God as a criminal trembles before the judge—the fear which mistrusts, suspects, and has no confidence in God—the fear which, therefore, keeps us away from God, causes us to dread the thought of drawing near to Him, and makes us say, like the fool to whom the psalmist refers, "No God." Many of you know what this kind of fear is, for you once suffered from it, though I trust you are now delivered from it by faith in Christ Jesus, and by the love which the Spirit of God has wrought in your hearts.

There is also another sort of fear which springs out of this slavish fear, and which is to be equally shunned; namely, a fear which leads to the apprehension that something evil is about to happen. There are many persons who have so little faith in God that they fear that the trials, which will sooner or later overtake them, will also overthrow them. They are afraid of a certain form of suffering that threatens them; they fear that they will not have patience enough to bear up under it; they feel sure that their spirit will sink in their sickness.

Above all, they are dreadfully afraid to die. They have not yet believed that God will be with them when they pass through the valley of death-shade, and because they cannot trust Him, they are all their lifetime subject to bondage. They cannot say that all things work together for good to them, but they often say, as poor old Jacob mistakenly said, "All these things are against me." And so they go on, fearing this and fearing that and fearing the other, and their life is spent, to a great extent, in sorrow and sighing.

May the Lord graciously deliver any of you who are in that condition! That is a kind of fear from which the true believer is free. He knows that whatever happens, God will overrule it for the good of His chosen.

"The Right Kind of Fear,"
Metropolitan Tabernacle Pulpit, No. 2971 (1876)

OUR INTERCESSOR

Peace I leave with you, my peace I give unto you: not as the world giveth, give I unto you. Let not your heart be troubled, neither let it be afraid.

JOHN 14:27

The Master displayed His love to His disciples throughout His life by the way in which He sought to comfort them when He foresaw that they would be cast down; especially was this true at the period before His passion—when one would have thought He might have sought for comfort, He was busy distributing it. Those choice words which have flown like a dove into many a mourner's window bearing the olive branch of peace were the fond utterances of a thoughtful heart.

Many such bottles of oil and wine did He apply to the wounds of His disciples. He would not have them suffer any kind of spiritual turmoil. "In the world ye shall have tribulation" said He, "but be of good cheer; I have overcome the world." His peace He distributed right liberally and left it as His last legacy: "Peace I leave with you, my peace I give unto you: not as the world giveth, give I unto you."

That He loved His disciples to the end is seen further in

the fact that He constantly pleaded for them when He poured out His strong cryings and tears. He watched them with an eye that was quick to perceive their perils, and before they knew their danger, He had already provided a refuge from it. Ere the poison was injected by the old serpent, the antidote was at hand. "Satan hath desired to have thee that he may sift thee as wheat." The temptation had not reached the stage of actual fact; it was only a desire on Satan's part, but the Lord outran the enemy with His intercessions and so saved poor Peter from the sieve.

The High Priest, chosen from among men, pleaded in His midnight wrestlings for all His people, mentioning their names one by one before the Majesty of heaven and so averting evils which otherwise had destroyed them. Surely those sacred pleadings brought down upon the apostolic band those matchless blessings which qualified them in after years to be the spiritual fathers of the church and the heralds of salvation to nations. Who doubts the love of such an Intercessor?

"THE FAITHFULNESS OF JESUS,"
METROPOLITAN TABERNACLE PULPIT, NO. 810 (1868)

COME UP HITHER

And they heard a great voice from heaven saying unto them, Come up hither. And they ascended up to heaven in a cloud; and their enemies beheld them.

REVELATION 11:12

The present is a shadow, a bubble that is dissolved; the future lasts forever. Where your treasure is, there let your heart be. Rejoice even now, I pray you, in your inheritance. As you are thus rich, let your spending money be dealt out with a generous hand. You are on your way to the mansions of the blessed; rejoice as you make the pilgrimage. If you have no present reason for thankfulness, yet the future may yield you much.

Break forth, therefore, into joy and singing, and with songs and everlasting joy upon your head make your way toward Zion. If it be so that all the future is yours, meditate much upon it; make heaven the subject of your daily thoughts; live not on this present, which is but food for swine, but live on the future, which is meat for angels. How refined will be your communications if your meditations are sublime! Your life will be heavenly if your musings are heavenly. Take wings to your spirit, and dwell among the angels.

All these things are yours; then prepare for them. Day by day, in the all-cleansing blood of Jesus which is the path of purity, wash your souls. By repentance cast off every sin; by a renewed application to Jesus and His Spirit, obtain fresh power against every evil. Stand ready for heaven with your loins girt about and your lamp trimmed; be waiting for the midnight cry, "Behold the bridegroom cometh!" Let your life be spent in the suburbs of the celestial city, in a devout sanctity of thought and act. Live upon the doorstep of the pearl gate, always waiting for the time when the angelic messenger shall say, "Come up hither."

Gratefully bless God that though thou deservest to descend into hell, thou hast such a place reserved for thee as heaven. Thou mightest have been cast away; the damnation of hell might have been thine only outlook; it is grace alone that has made thee to differ, and given thee a portion among them that are sanctified. Therefore bless God as long as thou hast any being, and let none hinder thee in thy sacred joy. Praise Him night and day for what He has done for thee.

"THINGS TO COME,"
METROPOLITAN TABERNACLE PULPIT, NO. 875 (1869)

WATCH AND WAIT

And account that the longsuffering of our Lord is salvation; even as our beloved brother Paul also according to the wisdom given unto him hath written unto you.

2 Peter 3:15

Why are His chariots so long in coming? Why does He delay? The world grows grey, not alone with age, but with iniquity; and yet the Deliverer comes not. We have waited for His footfall at the dead of night, and looked out for Him through the gates of the morning, and expected Him in the heat of the day, and reckoned that He might come ere yet another sun went down; but He is not here! He waits. He waits very, very long. Will He not come?

Longsuffering is that which keeps Him from coming. He is bearing with men. Not yet the thunderbolt! Not yet the riven heavens and the reeling earth! Not yet the great white throne and the day of judgment; for He is very pitiful and beareth long with men! Even to the cries of His own elect, who cry day and night unto Him—He is not in haste to answer, for He is very patient, slow to anger, and plenteous in mercy.

But His patience sometimes greatly puzzles us. We cannot

make it out. Eighteen, nineteen centuries, and the world not converted! Nineteen centuries, and Satan still to the front and all manner of iniquity still wounding this poor, bleeding world! What meaneth it? O Son of God, what meaneth it? Seed of the woman, when wilt Thou appear with Thy foot upon the serpent's head? We are puzzled at the longsuffering which causes so weary a delay.

A religion without mysteries seems to me to be false on the face of it. If there be an infinite God, it is not possible that poor I, with my finite mind, shall ever be able to understand everything about Him. If the Lord chooses to tarry till thousands of years have passed away—yea, till millions of years have elapsed—yet let Him do as He wills. Is He not infinitely wise and good, and who are we that we should put Him to the question? Let Him tarry His own time; only let us watch and wait, for He will come, and they that wait for Him shall have their reward.

"God's Long-suffering: An Appeal to the Conscience,"
Metropolitan Tabernacle Pulpit, No. 1997 (1886)

LOOK TO THE ROCK

For the Lord *shall comfort Zion: he will comfort all her waste places; and he will make her wilderness like Eden, and her desert like the garden of the* Lord*; joy and gladness shall be found therein, thanksgiving, and the voice of melody.*

Isaiah 51:3

It is therefore a dreadful thing when the Christian church begins to be discouraged, and means must be used to stay the evil. Such means we would use this day. Lo, we lift the standard of the divine promise. "Comfort ye, comfort ye, my people," sounds out like a silver trumpet in the front of the host. Be encouraged, O ye of the faint heart; there are no more difficulties now than there were of old. The cause is no more in jeopardy than it was a thousand years ago. The result, the end, the consummation of all things is absolutely certain: It is in His hand who cannot fail; therefore, be of good courage, and in waiting upon the Lord renew your strength.

Remember, ye that are cast down, that there are other voices besides those of the bittern and owl from the "waste places." You have listened long enough to dreary suggestions from within, to gloomy prophecies from desponding friends, to the taunts of foes, and to the horrible whisperings of Satan; now hearken to Him who promises to make the wilderness like Eden and the desert like the garden of the Lord.

O ye whose eyes are quick to discover evil, there are other sights in the world besides waste places and deserts, and hence my text hath near to it twice over the exhortation, *Look*—"Look unto the rock whence ye are hewn"; "Look unto Abraham your father" [Isaiah 51:1–2]. Why should your eyes forever ache over desolations? Probably you have seen as much in the wilderness as you are ever likely to see there. It does not take long to discover all the treasures and comforts of the burning sand; you have probably discovered them all by now. As for the discomforts and wants of the desert, you are perhaps as well acquainted with them as you need to be. Gaze no longer at the thirsty land and the burning sky; turn your eye where the finger of the Lord points by His Word.

"HEARKEN AND LOOK; OR, ENCOURAGEMENT FOR BELIEVERS,"
METROPOLITAN TABERNACLE PULPIT, NO. 1596 (1881)

JESUS LIVES

But he, being full of the Holy Ghost, looked up stedfastly into heaven, and saw the glory of God, and Jesus standing on the right hand of God,

ACTS 7:55

We are told that our Lord sits at the right hand of God "expecting till his enemies be made his footstool," and yet in the text He is not seen as sitting but as standing. Why standing? One of the old fathers says it was as though the Lord Jesus stood up in horror at the deed which was being done; as though He were about to interpose to help His servant die or to deliver Him out of their hands. He stands up, actively sympathizing with His suffering witness.

Well, beloved, this is just what we see in heaven. The Man of Sorrows is alive and sympathizes with His people still. Though raised to the throne of glory, He is not forgetful of our shame and sorrow. Think not, O child of earth, that the Son of Man has forgotten what temptation means and is now a stranger to human weakness and infirmity. "In all your affliction he is afflicted." He deeply sympathizes with every one of His tried brethren, "and in his measure feels afresh what every member bears."

Suppose not that He is an unthoughtful, uncaring spectator of your grief. I tell you, child of God, Christ has risen from His throne to succor you. He stands at this moment in the hour of your extremity, ready to help you. He will send you comforts when you need them, and He will see that your strength shall be to your day. What a sight was this for the dying Stephen! Jesus is living, and living with the same love in His heart which He showed on earth, with the same tender sympathy which He manifested among the twelve when He lingered among the sons of men.

The brightest point in the vision was this: He saw Jesus standing at the right hand of God. That was the point in dispute. The Jews said the Nazarene was an impostor. "No," said Stephen, "there He is; He stands at the right hand of God." To Stephen's mind the point was settled by what he saw. The people rage, the rulers take counsel together, but yonder is the King upon the holy hill of God; beyond a doubt He is a reigning monarch, and to Stephen's heart this was all he wished.

"STEPHEN'S MARTYRDOM,"
METROPOLITAN TABERNACLE PULPIT, NO. 740 (1867)

RUBBLE AND RESTORATION

Therefore thus saith the Lord G*OD, Behold, I lay in Zion for a foundation a stone, a tried stone, a precious corner stone, a sure foundation: he that believeth shall not make haste.*

ISAIAH 28:16

I can see a vast mass of ruins. Heaps upon heaps they lie around me. A stately edifice has tottered to the ground. Some terrible disaster has occurred. There it lies—cornice, pillar, pinnacle, everything of ornament and of utility—broken, scattered, dislocated. The world is strewn with the debris.

Journey where you will, the desolation is before your eyes. Who has done this? Who has cast down this temple? What hand has ruined this magnificent structure? Manhood, manhood it is which has been destroyed, and sin was the agent that effected the fall. It is man broken by his sin. Iniquity has done it. O thou devastator, what destructions hast thou wrought in the earth! What desolation thou hast made unto the ends of the world! Everywhere is ruin; everywhere is ruin. Futile attempts are made to rebuild this temple upon its own heap, and the Babel towers arise out of the rubbish and abide for a season, but they are soon broken down, and the mountain of decay and corruption becomes even more hopeless of restoration.

All that man has done with his greatest effort is but to make a huger display of his total failure to recover his position, to realize his ostentatious plans, or to restore his own fleeting memories of better things. They may build, and they may pile up stone upon stone, and cement them together with untempered mortar, but their rude structure shall all crumble to the dust again, for the first ruin will be perpetuated even to the last. So must it be, for sin destroys all. I am vexed in my spirit and sore troubled as I look at these ruins, fit habitations for the bittern and the dragon, the mole and the bat.

But what else do I see? I behold the great original builder coming forth from the ivory palaces to undo this mischief; and He cometh not with implements of destruction, that He may cast down and destroy every vestige, but I see Him advancing with plummet and line, that He may rear, set up, and establish on a sure foundation a noble pile that shall not crumble with time, but endure throughout all ages. He cometh forth with mercy.

"Maschil of Ethan, a Majestic Song,"
Metropolitan Tabernacle Pulpit, No. 1565 (1880)

GOD HAS FORESEEN

He that dwelleth in the secret place of the most High shall abide under the shadow of the Almighty. I will say of the Lord, He is my refuge and my fortress: my God; in him will I trust.

Psalm 91:1–2

Nothing shall happen to us which God has not foreseen. No unexpected event shall destroy His plans; no emergency shall transpire for which He has not provided; no peril shall occur against which He has not guarded. There shall come no remarkable want which shall take Him by surprise. He seeth the end from the beginning, and the things that are not, as though they were. To God's eye there is no past and no future. He fills His own eternal *now*; He stands in a position from which He can look down upon the whole, and see the past, the present, and the future at a single glance. All, all, all of the future is foreseen by Him and fixed by Him.

We may derive no small comfort from this fact. For suppose one goes to sea under the most skillful captain—that captain cannot possibly know what may occur during the voyage, and with the greatest foresight he can never promise an absolutely safe passage. There may be dangers which he has never yet encountered—Atlantic waves, tornadoes, and hurricanes that may yet sweep the good ship away, and they that sailed out of port merrily may never reach the haven. But when you come into the ship of Providence, He who is at the helm is the Master of every wind that shall blow and of every wave that shall break its force upon that ship; and He foresees as well the events that shall happen at the harbor for which we make, as those that happen at the port from which we start.

He knows in His own soul every wave with its height and breadth and force. He knows each wind; though the winds seem to be left without control, He knows each wind in all its connections and the speed at which each shall travel. How safe are we, then, when embarked in the good ship of Providence, with such a Captain who has fore-arranged and foreordained all things from the beginning even unto the end. And furthermore, how much it becomes us to put implicit confidence in His guidance!

"A Safe Prospective,"
Metropolitan Tabernacle Pulpit, No. 886 (1869)

LOOK UP

To give knowledge of salvation unto his people by the remission of their sins, through the tender mercy of our God; whereby the dayspring from on high hath visited us, to give light to them that sit in darkness and in the shadow of death, to guide our feet into the way of peace.

LUKE 1:77–79

It is a part of the tender mercy of our God that He visits those who despond and are motionless in a dread inactivity. Those who have lost hope are lost indeed, and such the Savior has come to save.

Then it is added, "and in the shadow of death." Did you ever feel that shadow? It has a horrible influence. Chill and cold, it freezes the marrow of the bones and stops the genial current of life in the veins. Death stands over the man, and if his hand does not smite, yet his shadow darkens joy and chills hope, benumbing the heart and making life itself a mode of death. The shadow of death is confusion of mind, depression of spirit, dread of the unknown, horror at the past, and terror of the future. Are any of you at this time bowing down under the shadow of death?

Has hell gaped wide and opened her jaws for you? Have you in your despair made a league with death and a covenant with hell? Thus saith the Lord, "Your covenant with death shall be disannulled, and your agreement with hell shall not stand"; for the Lord has come forth and visited you in the person of His dear Son to deliver the captive and save those who are appointed unto death. Knowing your guilt, the Lord visits you this morning, and bids you look up. "Behold the Lamb of God, which taketh away the sin of the world."

I do delight to think of this tender mercy of God to those who are lost. There are lost that shall be found, and last that shall be first. You seem forgotten of God, left out of the register of hope, but yet to you has Jesus come, "to give light to them that sit in darkness and in the shadow of death." Is not this tender mercy? If He had not come to shine on such I should never have been saved. A gospel for the cheerful would never have met my case; I wanted a gospel for the despairing.

"The Tender Mercy of Our God,"
Metropolitan Tabernacle Pulpit, No. 1907 (1886)

THE LORD REIGNS

Who knoweth not in all these that the hand of the Lord hath wrought this? In whose hand is the soul of every living thing, and the breath of all mankind.

Job 12:9–10

Thy life, thy death, thy prosperity in this world, thy growth in grace, thy peace—all things rest upon His sovereign will. Nothing can harm thee, unless He bids it. Nothing can cheer thee, unless He commands it. Thou resteth not in thine own hand. Be thy will never so headstrong, be thy mind never so stubborn, either thou must yield cheerfully or else thou must bend unwillingly. Thou art absolutely and entirely and in every respect placed at the will and disposal of Him who is thy God.

And now, child of God, let me ask thee this question: Art thou grieved because of this? Does this doctrine trouble thee? Let God lay aside His scepter; say, art thou prepared to wield it? Hadst thou rather have followed thine own will than be at God's disposal? Wouldst thou rather that He should be in everything and that He should do as He wills, or that it should be left to thee? Oh! I see ye, ye countless armies of God; I see ye bow your knees at once, and cry, "O Lord, we bless Thee that it is not so; we praise Thee that Thou hast left nothing to our disposal, but that Thou everywhere hast sway." This is not the subject of groaning but of mirth and joy to us. We set up our banners with this watchword: "The Lord reigneth."

We go on our journey with this as our constant cordial: "God is here." With this as our shield, we lift up our arm against calamity. With this as our sword, we rush into the thick of the battle against sin. If the book of my destiny were in my power today, I neither would erase a word nor insert a syllable. "Be it unto me even as thou wilt; not my will but thine be done." It is easy to say this, but oh, how hard to feel it when it comes to the trial hour. Take care, child of God, that thou holdest fast and firm this thy confidence, which shall have great recompence of reward.

"Everywhere and Yet Forgotten,"
New Park Street Pulpit, No. 326 (1860)

GOD STILL DOES WONDERS

For my thoughts are not your thoughts,
neither are your ways my ways, saith the Lord.

Isaiah 55:8

The Lord God does wonders still by maintaining His church and the cause of truth in the midst of the world. Read through history, and you meet with periods when the light seemed quenched; but then suddenly it burned up with superior luster. Remember the Reformation, and the revival of the last century. When spiritual life seemed almost extinct, there came times of refreshing from the presence of the Lord.

It will be the same at this dark hour. All the devils in hell can never quench the light of the truth. They may do all they can in union with all the wise men of the world to put down the old gospel of the cross; but even though they should slay it and bury it, it would rise again. When the voices which have been lifted up against the gospel shall have been silenced forever, the Word of the Lord shall sound forth to the ends of the earth. God is still doing great wonders in the maintenance of His despised gospel, and in the keeping alive of those spiritual doctrines which the carnal mind hates as much today as it ever did.

Now, dear brethren, why may we expect the Lord still to do wonders? Because His Word raises our expectations. Surely the Lord will not cease to work wonders and descend to the commonplace; for this Book talks of great things and marvelous things. Does He not say concerning His great grace, "As the heavens are higher than the earth, so are my ways higher than your ways, and my thoughts than your thoughts"? Have we not many passages of scripture which run in this wise: "Though your sins be as scarlet they shall be as white as snow"? The universe is challenged by the question, "Who is a God like unto thee, that pardoneth iniquity, and passeth by the transgression of the remnant of his heritage?" Hear our Lord speak and invite the laboring and heavy laden to His rest. Hear Him declare that "All manner of sin and blasphemy shall be forgiven unto men."

"God the Wonder-worker,"
Metropolitan Tabernacle Pulpit, No. 1981 (1887)

HOPE OF BETTER DAYS

For she said, If I may touch but his clothes, I shall be whole.

MARK 5:28

For twelve years it appears she had persevered, in different ways and in the teeth of terrible agonies. We are told that she had suffered many things of many physicians. It is bad enough to suffer many things of one surgeon, but she had suffered many things from many practitioners.

The physicians of those days were a great deal more to be dreaded than the worst diseases. If I were now to read to you even a brief account of the surgery practiced in olden times, you would shudder and beg me to close the book. Any reasonable person might prefer to suffer from any form of natural disorder rather than submit himself to the hands of the doctors of those days. What with cupping, leeching and cutting, cauterizing, blistering and incision, strapping, puncturing, and putting in setons, patients were made to undergo all manner of unimaginable tortures.

I admire this woman's marvelous hopefulness. She still believes that she can be cured. She ought to have given up the idea long ago according to the ordinary processes of reasoning;

for generally we put several instances together, and from these several instances we deduce a certain inference. Now she might have put the many physicians together, and their many failures, and have rationally inferred that her case was past hope. She might have said, "My disease is incurable. I must ask for patience to bear it till I die, but no longer dream of a cure." But no, bright-eyed woman as I have no doubt she was, she saw hope where others would have despaired.

Something within her buoyed her up, and she still had hopes of better days—and so, when she heard of Jesus, her heart leaped within her. Her hope said, "The blessing has come at last. I have long waited for it, and now God has sent it to me. Here it is; and I will seize it at once. Now has the sun of righteousness arisen upon me with healing beneath His wings, and I will bathe in His sunlight. Now I have escaped from mere pretenders, and I have found one who has real power to heal." You see, then, the patient. A woman of spirit, of resolution, and of hopefulness. Such persons make grand workers when they are converted.

"THE TOUCH,"
METROPOLITAN TABERNACLE PULPIT, NO. 1382 (1877)

THE PATH OF LIFE

Thou wilt shew me the path of life: in thy presence is fulness of joy; at thy right hand there are pleasures for evermore.

PSALM 16:11

Here is as brief and yet complete a description of heaven as I can well give you. The things to come thus mentioned belong to all the saints; life is yours—not mere existence, but life fraught with happiness and bliss. Life and the path of it—that mysterious secret which only Jesus could reveal. That narrow path the eagle's eye hath not seen and the lion's whelp hath not trodden; it is the secret of the Lord which is with them that fear Him. But that path of life is yours today!

Think of it! Christ in you is that path of life—He is yours! The life eternal is in you now. The life of heaven is none other than the life of believers developed. "I give unto my sheep eternal life"; they have it now, the selfsame life that suns itself in the presence of God is the life which reveals itself this day in prayer, which groans in desire, and which sings with holy joy in gratitude to the Most High.

You have already then, as yours, the life and the path of life, which constitute heaven. "In thy presence," says the psalmist; the divine presence is heaven; to see the face of God, to be consciously and acceptably near to God; no longer set afar off by sin or divided by frailty or aught besides; this is our glorious rest. But, beloved, ours is this divine presence today; according as we are able to bear it, we behold the face of our Father now. Though, by reason of our mortality, we could not endure to behold His unclouded splendor; yet, in the person of Jesus Christ, the Mediator, we perceive the brightness of the Father's glory.

Heaven, in the text, is described as nearness to God, in the words, "At thy right hand." How near the glorified are in heaven they themselves know; but we are near also; and though not always near to our own perception, yet faith rejoices that the justified are a people near unto God—as near, indeed, as Christ Himself is.

"Things to Come,"
Metropolitan Tabernacle Pulpit, No. 875 (1869)

THE LONG, TEDIOUS WINTER

Be patient therefore, brethren, unto the coming of the Lord. Behold, the husbandman waiteth for the precious fruit of the earth, and hath long patience for it, until he receive the early and latter rain.

JAMES 5:7

If he has sown in the winter, he does not expect he will reap in the early spring; he does not go forth with his sickle in the month of May and expect to find golden sheaves. He waits. The moons wax and wane; suns rise and set; but the husbandman waits till the appointed time is come. Wait thou, O sufferer, till the night be over. Watch after watch thou hast already passed through; the morning breaketh. Tarry thou a little longer, for if the vision tarry it shall come. "Thou shalt stand in thy lot in the end of the days." Ere long thou shalt have a happy exit out of thy present trials.

Are you a worker? Then you need as much patience in working as you do in suffering. We must not expect to see immediate results in all cases from the preaching of the gospel, from the teaching of scripture in our classes, from distributing religious literature, or from any other kind of effort.

Immediate results may come. Sometimes they do, and they greatly cheer the worker; but it is given to some to wait long, like the husbandman, ere the fruit reaches maturity.

Truth is mighty and it will prevail, though it may have a hard fight before it wins the victory. Souls may not be won to God the first time you pray for them, nor the first time you exhort them—nay, nor the twentieth time. If thou hast gone to a sinner once on Christ's errand and he has rejected thee, go again seven times—nay, go again seventy times seven; for if thou shouldst at last succeed by thy Master's gracious help, it will well repay thee.

The long, tedious winter of thy waiting will appear as a short span to look back upon when thou hast reaped the field of thy labor. The little patience that thou hadst to exert for a while will seem as nothing, like the travail of the mother when the man-child is born into the world. Hush, then, your sad complaints, and still your petulant wailings.

"A Visit to the Harvest Field,"
Metropolitan Tabernacle Pulpit, No. 1025 (1871)

COMFORT FOR YOUR SPIRIT

Fear thou not; for I am with thee: be not dismayed; for I am thy God: I will strengthen thee; yea, I will help thee; yea, I will uphold thee with the right hand of my righteousness.

ISAIAH 41:10

If there should be nothing in the sermon this evening, brethren, there is enough in the text to satisfy your mouth with good things, so that your youth may be renewed like the eagle's. May the Holy Spirit spread for you a table in the wilderness, and give you appetites to feed by faith upon these royal dainties, which, like the vegetables that Daniel and his companions fed upon, shall make you well favored before God and man.

To whom are these words spoken? For we must not steal from God's scripture any more than from man's treasury. We have no more right to take a promise for ourselves that does not belong to us than we have to take another man's purse from him. These words were evidently spoken in God's name by the prophet to God's "chosen" ones. Read the eighth verse: "But you, Israel, are my servant, Jacob whom *I have chosen*, the seed of Abraham my friend." And again in the ninth verse: "You are my servant; I have *chosen* you." So, then, if you or I should find anything that is gracious and comforting here it will come to us, not upon the footing of merit but upon the basis of sovereign grace. It will not be ours because we have chosen Christ, but because He has chosen us.

Our heavenly Father has blessed us with all spiritual blessings according as He has chosen us in Christ Jesus from before the foundation of the world. The eternal choice is the wellhead from which all the springs of mercy flow. Happy are you, my soul, if grace has inscribed your name in God's eternal book! You may come to this text, like a child to his father's own table, and you may draw from it all manner of comforts to sustain your spirit.

"Away with Fear,"
Metropolitan Tabernacle Pulpit, No. 930 (1870)

TO BE AT PEACE

Cast thy burden upon the Lord, and he shall sustain thee: he shall never suffer the righteous to be moved.

Psalm 55:22

When a man stays himself upon God it is not only his faith that brings him peace, but his faith is rewarded by peace, which the Lord gives him as a token of approval. A kind of discipline is going on in our heavenly Father's family—not rewards and punishments such as judges award to criminals, but such as fathers give to their children. By this we are being trained for the many mansions in the Father's house above. If we will stay ourselves on God, we shall have peace; if we will not do so, we shall have no rest, but shall be in sore disquietude.

The pressure of the trouble comes with the decline of faith. If thou believest more, it may not make thee richer but thou wilt not feel thy poverty so keenly. If thou believest more, it may not make thee healthy in body but thou shalt not fret because of thy sickness: If thou believest more, it will not give thee back thy buried ones but it shall fill thy heart with a still higher love. "All things are possible to him that believeth," and peace, peace is among those possibilities; but if thou wilt not believe, neither shalt thou be established. Thine unbelief shall be a rod for thine own back, a bitter for thine own cup. If thou wilt not trust thy God, thou shalt wander into a weary land, seeking rest and finding none. Come, brothers and sisters, let us fly from such a fate and win perfect peace as the reward of perfect confidence.

You have lost one that was very dear to you, and instead of fretting and repining, you kiss the hand of God and go about your daily duties with patience. That is a very wonderful fruit of the Spirit, wrought by faith—and thus faith is seen. A man has had a fire, or some other form of loss, and his comforts are destroyed. If he is an unbeliever, we do not wonder that he tears his hair and curses God and rages and fumes. But if he has stayed himself on God, he will be at peace.

"The Song of a City and the Pearl of Peace,"
Metropolitan Tabernacle Pulpit, No. 1818 (1885)

GREAT REWARD FOR PERSECUTION

Blessed are they which are persecuted for righteousness' sake: for theirs is the kingdom of heaven. Blessed are ye, when men shall revile you, and persecute you, and shall say all manner of evil against you falsely, for my sake. Rejoice, and be exceeding glad: for great is your reward in heaven: for so persecuted they the prophets which were before you.

MATTHEW 5:10–12

Men meditate mischief, but it miserably miscarries. God grants protection to the persecuted, and provides an escape from the most perilous exposure. Full often the darkest conspiracy is brought to the direst confusion. No sooner does Christ gather a church in any place, be it a renowned empire or a paltry village, than opposition is stirred up. "If ye were of the world, the world would love his own: but because ye are not of the world, but I have chosen you out of the world, therefore the world hateth you." "I will put enmity between thee and the woman, and between thy seed and her seed," is the first check for the serpent's wiles, the first ray of hope for his helpless victims; and the prediction will continue to be fulfilled till at last, according to the word of the Lord, the tares are bound in bundles to burn them and the wheat is gathered into His garner.

Whenever there has been a great persecution raised against the Christian church, God has overruled it, as He did in the case of Pharaoh's oppression of the Israelites, by making the aggrieved community more largely to increase. The early persecutions in Judea promoted the spread of the gospel; hence, when after the death of Stephen the disciples were all scattered abroad throughout the regions of Judea and Samaria, except the apostles, the result is thus given: "Therefore they that were scattered abroad went everywhere preaching the word."

So too when Herod stretched forth his hands to vex certain of the church and killed James, the brother of John, with the sword, what came of it? Why Luke tells us in almost the same words that Moses had used: "The word of God grew and multiplied." Those terrible and bloody persecutions under the Roman emperor by no means stayed the progress of the gospel but strangely enough seemed to press forward for the crown of martyrdom.

The church probably never increased at a greater ratio than as when her foes were most fierce to assail and most resolute to destroy her.

"Prosperity Under Persecution,"
Metropolitan Tabernacle Pulpit, No. 997 (1871)

CHANGE SHOULD BE EXPECTED

While the earth remaineth, seedtime and harvest, and cold and heat, and summer and winter, and day and night shall not cease.

GENESIS 8:22

While the earth remains there will be changes in the spiritual world. Read the text laying a stress upon the words of change, and see how it rises and falls like the waves of the sea: "While the earth remains, *seedtime* and *harvest*, and *cold* and *heat*, and *summer* and *winter*, and *day* and *night* shall not cease." Not one of these states continues; it comes and goes. The seasons are a perpetual procession, an endless chain, an ever-moving wheel. Cold flies before heat, and soon summer is chased away by winter. Nothing is stable.

Such is this life; such are the feelings of spiritual life with most men, such is the history of the church of God. We sorrow and we rejoice; we struggle and we triumph; we labor and we rest. We are not long upon Tabor, neither are we always in the valley of Baca. Let us not be amazed, as though some strange thing happened to us, if our day darkens into night, or our summer chills into winter. From joy to sorrow, from sorrow to joy, from success to defeat, from defeat to success, we pass very rapidly. It is so: It will be so while the earth remains, and we remain partakers of the earth.

Yet, there will be an order in it all. Cold and heat, and summer and winter, and day and night do not come in a giddy dance or tumultuous hurry-burly, but they make up the fair and beautiful year. Chance has no part in these affairs. God compels winds and storms and sun and sea to keep the order of His house, and none rebels against His commandment. So in the spiritual kingdom, in the life of the believer, and in the history of the church of God, all things are made to work for good, and the spiritual is being educated into the heavenly. In our seasons there is an order visible to God, even when we walk in darkness and see no light. We have our winters, in which the sap is prepared in secret to produce the clusters of summer; we have our colds, in which we lose the superfluities bred of our heat. Expect the changes, and believe that they come by rule.

"The Sermon of the Seasons,"
Metropolitan Tabernacle Pulpit, No. 1891 (1886)

GROWING IN GRACE

For he shall deliver the needy when he crieth;
the poor also, and him that hath no helper.

PSALM 72:12

When a Christian is richest in grace he is poorest in himself. The way to grow rich in grace is to feel your poverty. Whenever you think you have stored up a little strength, a little comfort, a little provision against a rainy day, you are pretty sure to have the trouble you bargained for and to miss the resources you counted on. Estimate your true wealth before God by your entire dependence on Him. The more you have, the less you have, and the less you have, the more you have. When you have nothing at all in yourself, then Christ is all in all to you.

The perpetual condition of every child of God in himself is that of a needy and a poor and a helpless one—on the high mountains with his Lord, rejoicing in His love, yet he is even there in himself less than nothing and vanity—still poor and needy.

There have been times when we felt this very powerfully, perhaps very painfully. Has Satan ever beset you, my brethren, with his fierce temptations? No doubt many of you have had to feel the ferocity of his attacks. Perhaps blasphemous thoughts have been injected into your mind—dark forebodings, such as these: "God has forsaken me." Perhaps he has said, "He has sinned himself out of the covenant—he is a castaway," and your poor little faith has tried to hold on to Christ but it seemed as if she must be driven from her hold. While others found it, as you thought, easy to get to heaven, you realized the truth of the text, "The righteous scarcely are saved."

You have had to fight for every inch of ground, and it seemed to you often as though you had not a spark of grace in you, not a ray of hope, and not so much as a single grain of the grace of God within your heart. Ah! And at such times you have been poor and needy and you have had no helper. And, perhaps, at such seasons too, temporal trouble may have come in. Whoever may go through the world without trouble, God's people never do.

"THE POOR MAN'S FRIEND,"
METROPOLITAN TABERNACLE PULPIT, NO. 1037 (1872)

LIVE BY FAITH

Thou wilt keep him in perfect peace, whose mind is stayed on thee: because he trusteth in thee.

ISAIAH 26:3

No man can be said to be at perfect peace who has any cause of disquietude at all. Yet the child of God has this perfect peace according to our Lord's own statement; and therefore, it must be true that the believer is raised above all disquietude.

"What," say you, "has he not an evil heart of unbelief?" Yes, and that demands his watchfulness, but should not create in him any kind of terror; for "God is greater than our hearts," and where sin abounded, grace doth much more abound. The flesh has received its death warrant, and unbelief is but a part of the flesh doomed to die. The holy life within us must triumph. "If we believe not, yet he abideth faithful: he cannot deny himself." Though we be as yet like the smoking flax, we shall soon shine forth, and He will bring forth judgment unto victory.

"Ah," saith one, "but I have disquietude in my family; I have a wild, unruly son," or "I have a sick, pining child, who will soon be taken away from me by consumption!" Yes, friend, but if your mind is stayed on God and you can trust God with such matters, you should not lose your perfect peace even through this. For what if your heart be troubled? Will that make the consumptive child any stronger? Or will your melancholy be likely to restrain your rebellious son? No, but "the just shall live by faith," and shall triumph by faith too.

It shall be your strength to bring your sick and lay them at Jesus' feet; it shall be your hope to bring your unruly one and say, "Lord, cast out the devil from my child, and let him live unto Thee." Nothing ought to avail to break the peace of the believer; the shield of faith should quench every fiery dart.

Observe that Christ has taken possession of you, and you are His; neither will He lose you, but He will hold you singlehanded against the world and death and hell. Observe too that your heavenly Father rules in providence, giving you what you need, for He has said, "No good thing will I withhold from them that walk uprightly."

"The Song of a City and the Pearl of Peace,"
Metropolitan Tabernacle Pulpit, No. 1818 (1885)

A WORD FOR THE PERSECUTED

Let us hold fast the profession of our faith without wavering; (for he is faithful that promised).

HEBREWS 10:23

It is as well when you have medicine to give to a child to show him a piece of sugar too; so let your kindness and cheerfulness and gentleness sweeten that which the world is not very likely to receive anyhow, but which it will the less resent if you present it with love, showing a desire to live peaceably with all men and to consult the comfort of others rather than your own. And then endure whatever you have to endure with the greatest possible meekness.

There was a farmer whose wife was very irritated with him because of his attending a dissenting place of worship and joining with Christian people. She often declared that she would not bear it much longer, but he was very patient and made no harsh reply to her. One day she fetched him out of the harvest field and said, "Now it is come to this; you will give up those people or give me up." And she brought out a web of cloth and said, "Now you take half of this and I'll take the other half; for I am going."

He said, "No, my dear, you are welcome to it all. You have always been a very good industrious wife—take it all." Then she proposed taking a part of their household goods and settling everything for a final separation, but again he said, "Take all there is. If you will go away take everything you like, for I should not wish you to be uncomfortable; and come back again whenever you please. I shall always be glad to see you."

Seeing that he talked in that way, she said, "Do you mean me to go?"

"No," said he, "it is your own wish, not mine. I cannot give up my religion, but anything else I can do to make you stay and be happy, I will do." This was too much for her; she resolved to cease her opposition, and in a short time went with her husband to the place of worship and became herself a believer.

This is the surest way to victory. Yield everything but what it would be wrong to yield. Never grow angry. Keep cool, and let the railing be all on one side.

"A Word for the Persecuted,"
Metropolitan Tabernacle Pulpit, No. 1188 (1874)

PERFECT PEACE

Thou wilt keep him in perfect peace, whose mind is stayed on thee: because he trusteth in thee.

ISAIAH 26:3

Let the peace of God decide for you in all trials of temper, and endurings of wrong, and questions which lead to debate and separation. Set peace in the chariot, and let it hold the reins; for anger will, like Phaeton of old, set the world on fire. Oh, Peace of God, rule thou me!

Pray God that the power of this peace may be constantly upon you. If you lose your peace with God you lose your power to judge under difficulties; you lose your power of self-control under provocations; you lose the best sovereign that ever held a scepter. I believe that if a man is walking with God in the light, and enjoying full fellowship with heaven, he may go down into any meeting, however turbulent—into any society, however discordant the elements may be—and yet he will be wise to answer, wise to be silent, wise to do, or wise not to do; for the peace of God will keep him calm and quiet.

Once let the mind be thoroughly disturbed and unhinged before the Lord, and you are weak as another man—and you say that which you will have to unsay, and you do that which you would wish to wipe out with your tears. When rest of soul is gone, hard things are spoken and hard things are done, which would not consort with communion with the tender Lord. Let the peace of God always rule, or otherwise you will not always be safe. Especially let the peace of God rule your affections.

Be satisfied that you love God, and that your heart cleaves to God and does not follow after any other. Be at peace with God as to your heart and, when that is so and the affections are dominated by conscious love to God, it is then that you fight the battles of life with comfort to yourself and with honor to the name of Him to whom you belong.

Remember, you can only yourself be happy in heart and healthy in spirit as long as you keep the peace of God. You are sure to become wretched and unhappy, you are sure to stumble here and there into faults, if that peace of God be gone.

"That Horrible East Wind!"
Metropolitan Tabernacle Pulpit, No. 1693 (1882)

GOD'S OATH

These things I have spoken unto you, that in me ye might have peace. In the world ye shall have tribulation: but be of good cheer; I have overcome the world.

JOHN 16:33

Were you not cold on your way hither this morning? Did you not see the snow upon the ground, and do you dare to doubt God? He hath said, "While the earth remaineth, seed time and harvest, summer and winter, cold and heat shall never cease"; and He keeps His word. And yet you think, though He keeps that word, He will forget the word that He has spoken concerning you.

You come here in trouble this morning. Do you not see that God is true? That your very trouble is a proof that He has not forsaken you? If you never had any trouble, then God would have broken His promise, for did not Jesus Christ leave you it as a legacy? "In the world ye shall have tribulation." There, you have got it. That proves that God is true. Now, you have a part of the legacy, you shall have the rest: "In the world ye shall have tribulation, but be of good cheer; I have overcome the world."

So that the very weather without, and your troubles within, ought to forbid your doubting the faithfulness of your God. But look here: Has not God made you a promise, saying, "I will never leave thee nor forsake thee"? Would you like to be called a promise breaker? Shall I point my finger at you and say, "There's a man whose word is not to be relied on"? Will you point that same finger to God and say, "His word is not to be taken; He is not to be trusted"? What! Do you think your God is dishonorable? That He will give a promise and break it? Not keep it? Forget it? Fail to remember it? What! God, the God of glory, prove dishonorable? It must not, cannot be.

Recollect, again, He has given you His oath. Can you think that He will break that? Because He could swear by no greater, He swore by Himself. Shall God be perjured? You would not think that of your meanest fellow creature; will you think that of your greatest and best friend?

"Dilemma and Deliverance,"
New Park Street Pulpit, No. 287 (1859)

AFFLICTIONS ARE PROOF OF SONSHIP

And even to your old age I am he; and even to hoar hairs will I carry you: I have made, and I will bear; even I will carry, and will deliver you.

Isaiah 46:4

Let me have your reasons you think you shall never ascend the hill of God. The first reply is, "I shall never get there, for I am weak, and the hill is exceeding high; and, sir, you have told us that godliness is a great steep and that true religion is a towering up, and I am so weak; to will is present with me, but how to perform I find not. I can do nothing, I am emptied entirely, I know that this can never be performed by me. To perfect holiness and perfect rest I can never come, for I am the weakest of the entire family, and that steep is too lofty to be attained by tottering feet like mine. My bones ache, my knees bend, hot sweat drenches my garments, my head is giddy, and I drag my bleeding feet with anguish from crag to crag."

It is true the hill is steep, but then God is omnipotent. It is certain that the Alp is high, but higher still is the love and grace of God. He hath borne you, He hath carried you, and

He will carry you even to the end. When you cannot walk He will take you in His arms, and when the road is so rough that you cannot even creep along it, He will bear you as on eagles' wings till He bring you to His promised rest. If it were yourself that you had to look to, it would be right in you to mourn—but you are not to look to self. Trust thou in the Lord forever, for in the Lord Jehovah is everlasting strength.

If your road were smooth, you might fear that you were like the wicked who stand in slippery places. Because your pathway is rough, the better foothold for a mountain climber. There is nothing so much to be feared as that smooth glass-faced rock on which the foot slips back and slides. No, those stones and flints give foothold. Stand then, strong in the strength of God, and be of good courage. Your affliction are proofs of your sonship.

"Climbing the Mountain,"
Metropolitan Tabernacle Pulpit, No. 396 (1861)

A VISIT FROM THE KING

What is man, that thou art mindful of him?
and the son of man, that thou visitest him?

PSALM 8:4

Observe that God has not merely pitied us from a distance and sent us relief by way of the ladder which Jacob saw, but He hath Himself visited us. It needs no studied language to preach from this text; the expressions themselves are full of holy thought. A visit from God, what must it be! "Lord, what is man, that thou art mindful of him? and the son of man, that thou visitest him?"

A visit from the queen would be remembered by most of you all your lives; you would feel yourselves half ennobled But a visit from God, what shall I say of it? That He should stoop to leave His high abode and the majesty wherein He reigns to visit insignificant beings like ourselves? This Bible is a letter from Him, and we prize it beyond the finest gold; but an actual visit from God Himself, what shall we say of such a favor? In what ways has the Lord shown His tender mercy in deigning to visit us?

I answer, first, God's great visit to us is the incarnation of our blessed Lord and Savior Jesus Christ. Many visits of God to men had been paid before that—read your Bibles, and see; but the most wonderful visit of all was when He came to tarry here, some thirty years and more, to work out our salvation. What but tender mercy, hearty mercy, intense mercy, could bring the great God to visit us so closely that He actually assumed our nature?

Kings may visit their subjects, but they do not think of taking upon themselves their poverty, sickness, or sorrow. They could not if they would, and would not if they could; this were more than we could expect from them. But our divine Lord, when He came hither, came into our flesh. He veiled His godhead in a robe of our inferior clay. O children! The Lord so visited you as to become a babe, and then a child who dwelt with His parents and was subject unto them, and grew in stature as you must do. O working men! The Lord so visited you as to become the carpenter's son and to know all about your toil and your weariness—ay, even to hunger and faintness.

"The Tender Mercy of God,"
Metropolitan Tabernacle Pulpit, No. 1907 (1886)

STAY YOURSELF ON GOD

Now the God of hope fill you with all joy and peace in believing, that ye may abound in hope, through the power of the Holy Ghost.

ROMANS 15:13

Of this be ye well assured: Your souls are on the wing and are bound to fly on and on forever unless they make bold to settle down upon the Lord their God. In God is rest, but in none else. All earth and heaven, time and eternity, cannot make up a peace for a bruised spirit—and yet a word from the Lord bestows it beyond recall.

Let us commit ourselves, and all that we are, and all that we have, and all that we have to do, and all that we have to suffer, to the guardian care of our loving God, casting all our care upon Him, for He careth for us. Here we are in God, and here we mean to abide. We are not regretting the grace of yesterday, nor sighing for the grace of tomorrow. We stay where we are—at home with God. Our anchor is down, and we do not mean to draw it up again. "My heart is fixed, O God, my heart is fixed: I will sing and give praise."

"Oh," saith one, "you do not know my troubles!" No, but

I remember the story of a poor Methodist at the battle of Fontenoy. He had both his legs shot away, and when the surgeon came to attend to him, he was evidently bleeding to death—but he cried, "I am as happy as I can be out of Paradise!" Well, if in the very article of death, and suffering as he was, he could overflow with happiness, surely you and I can rejoice in perfect peace.

I want you all to be like Dr. Watts, who said that for many years he went to his bed without the slightest solicitude as to whether he should wake up in this world or in the next. To rest in God's Word, to rejoice in God's covenant, to trust in the divine sacrifice, to be conformed to God's will, to delight in God's self—this is to stay yourself upon God, and the consequence of it is perfect peace.

"The Song of a City, and the Pearl of Peace,"
Metropolitan Tabernacle Pulpit, No. 1818 (1885)

YOUR STRONGHOLD

The Lord is good, a strong hold in the day of trouble; and he knoweth them that trust in him.

Nahum 1:7

Have you read this chapter through? It is a very terrible one; it is like the rushing of a mighty river when it is nearing a cataract. It boils and seethes and flows with overwhelming force, bearing everything before it, yet right in the middle of the surging flood stands out, like a green island, this most cheering, comforting, and delightful text.

Listen a minute to the prophet's words of terror. "The Lord is slow to anger, and great in power, and will not at all acquit the wicked: the Lord hath his way in the whirlwind and in the storm, and the clouds are the dust of his feet. He rebuketh the sea, and maketh it dry, and drieth up all the rivers: Bashan languisheth, and Carmel, and the flower of Lebanon languisheth. The mountains quake at him, and the hills melt, and the earth is burned at his presence, yea, the world, and all that dwell therein. Who can stand before his indignation? and who can abide in the fierceness of his anger? his fury is poured out like fire, and the rocks are thrown down by him."

Then, just as there has sometimes been a break and a delightful silence in the very midst of some tremendous chorus of sacred song, so here the thunder pauses, the hurricane is stopped, and we hear the sweet music of this still small voice: "JEHOVAH is good, a strong hold in the day of trouble; and he knoweth them that trust in him"—from which we may gather that there is always a hiding place for His people. His eyes of love are fixed on them even when they flash fire upon His adversaries. Nothing shall harm them, though the earth be removed and the mountains are cast into the midst of the sea; they may rejoice in the goodness of the Lord in the day of His fierce anger.

"THE STRONGHOLD,"
METROPOLITAN TABERNACLE PULPIT, NO. 2555 (1883)

PEACE: HOW GAINED

I will hear what God the Lord will speak: for he will speak peace unto his people, and to his saints: but let them not turn again to folly.

Psalm 85:8

The psalmist had been praying. At the mercy seat he had spread out this petition: "Wilt thou not revive us again: that thy people may rejoice in thee? Show us thy mercy, O Lord, and grant us thy salvation." When he had spoken, he desired an answer. He watched and waited till the Lord God should give him a reply.

A friend, kindly wishing to spare me, puts at the end of his letter, "No answer expected." This is too often a footnote to men's prayers. David did not pray in that fashion; he did expect an answer from the mouth of the Lord. He said within himself, "I have spoken; but now I will speak no more but hear what God the Lord will speak."

Always follow up prayer with holy expectancy. Prayers which expect no answer are guilty of taking the name of God in vain; they are a misuse of the holy ordinance of supplication; and they are a question put upon the divine existence, inasmuch as they reduce the godhead to an idol, like to those images of the heathen which have ears but they hear not, neither speak they through their throats. Prayers without faith are an insult to the attributes of God, and do dishonor to His sacred name. If thou prayest aright, in the name of Jesus, expect the Lord to hear thee, even as thou wouldst hear thy child if he asked bread of thee.

It should be the daily resolve of every Christian man—"I will hear what God the LORD will speak." Not only when I am dazed and confused with other voices, nor only when I have expressed my heart in prayer, but at all times and seasons, I will hear what God the Lord shall speak.

There are many doctrines and controversies; but "I will hear what God the LORD will speak." His voice, by His prophets and apostles, shall be the umpire of every dispute with me. I will also turn to the Word of God for the rule of my daily life, as well as for the instruction of my mind in doctrine. I will have regard to the precepts as well as to the promises.

"PEACE: HOW GAINED, HOW BROKEN,"
METROPOLITAN TABERNACLE PULPIT, NO. 2112 (1889)

NO SMOOTH PATHWAYS

As it is written, For thy sake we are killed all the day long; we are accounted as sheep for the slaughter. Nay, in all these things we are more than conquerors through him that loved us.

ROMANS 8:36–37

The apostle gives us a little summary of the evils with which we must fight, and he places first, tribulation. The word *tribulation* in the Latin signifies threshing, and God's people are often cast upon the threshing floor to be beaten with the heavy flail of trouble; but they are more than conquerors, since they lose nothing but their straw and chaff, and the pure wheat is thus separated from that which was of no benefit to it.

The original Greek word, however, suggests pressure from without. It is used in the case of persons who are bearing heavy burdens and are heavily pressed upon. Now, believers have had to contend with outward circumstances more or less in all ages. At the present day, there are very few who do not at some time or other in their lives meet with outward pressure, either from sickness, or from loss of goods, or from bereavements, or from some other of the thousand and one causes from which affliction springs.

The Christian has not a smooth pathway. "In the world, ye shall have tribulation" is a sure promise which never fails of fulfilment. But under all burdens, true believers have been sustained; no afflictions have ever been able to destroy their confidence in God.

It is said of the palm tree that the more weights they hang upon it the more straight and the more lofty doth it tower towards heaven; and it is so with the Christian. Like Job, he is never so glorious as when he has passed through the loss of all things, and at last rises from his dunghill more mighty than a king.

Brethren, you must expect to meet with this adversary so long as you are here; and if you now suffer the pressure of affliction, remember you must overcome it and not yield to it. Cry unto the strong for strength, that your tribulation may work out for you patience, and patience experience, and experience hope that maketh not ashamed.

"More Than Conquerors,"
Metropolitan Tabernacle Pulpit, No. 751 (1867)

LET CHRIST REIGN

Wherefore God also hath highly exalted him, and given him a name which is above every name: that at the name of Jesus every knee should bow, of things in heaven, and things in earth, and things under the earth; and that every tongue should confess that Jesus Christ is Lord, to the glory of God the Father.

PHILIPPIANS 2:9–11

This doctrine has been to my own soul the only one which has cheered me in times of extremely deep depression of spirit. As I have told you before, so I tell you now—I have known what it is to be brought so low in heart that no promise of God's Word gave me a ray of light, nor a single doctrine afforded me a gleam of comfort; and yet, so often as I have come across this text, "Wherefore God also hath highly exalted him, and given him a name which is above every name," I have always found a flood of joy bursting into my soul, for I have said, "Well, it is of no consequence what may become of me if my name be cast out as evil, and if I myself am left in darkness; if pains should multiply; if sorrows should increase beyond number, it does not matter—I will not lift up a finger so long as my Lord Jesus is exalted."

I believe that every genuine Christian heart that loves the Savior feels just that, like the dying soldier in the hour of battle, who is cheered with the thought, "The general is safe; the victory is on our side; my blood is well spent, my life well lost, to win the victory."

Let Christ reign, and I will make no bargain with God as to myself. Let Jesus be king the whole world over; I care for nothing else. Let Him wear the crown; let the pleasure of the Lord prosper in His hands; let His covenant purposes be fulfilled; let His elect be saved; let the kingdoms of this world become the kingdoms of our Lord and of His Christ. Why, what mattereth it even though ten thousand of us should go pining through the valley of the shadow of death? Our lives and deaths were all well spent to earn so great a reward as to see Jesus glorified.

"STEPHEN'S MARTYRDOM,"
METROPOLITAN TABERNACLE PULPIT, NO. 740 (1867)

HEAVEN IS JUST AHEAD

His servants shall serve him: And they shall see his face.

Revelation 22:3–4

The time comes when this mortal life shall be utterly swallowed up in life eternal. Let me suggest to you, my beloved brothers and sisters, that we think much about the life to come. We shall soon be there in the endless home; let us send our thoughts thither like couriers in advance. Let the harps of angels ring out their music to our listening ears; let the songs of the redeemed awaken us to unite with them in the praises of our Lord. You will soon be there; anticipate the joy.

Put on your white robes by faith, and even if a little imagination should come to the aid of faith it will do no harm. Your heads will soon wear the crown—the crown which you will delight to cast at Jesus' feet. Today you know the straits of poverty, but you are going where the streets are paved with transparent gold. You now know the aches and pains of this frail flesh, but you are going where perpetual youth and vigor shall cause all pain to flee away. You are passing quickly along the journey; think much of that journey's end. Remember the rest which remaineth, the perfection which is promised, the victory which is secured, the communion which is provided, the glory which is dawning. "His servants shall serve him, and they shall see his face." Think much of your home: Every good child will do so.

When you think of it, and your heart grows warm with the thought, then count it very near. Suppose you are to live a comparatively long life, yet no human life is really long. Even to a young man, if he has to look forward to a grey old age, life is but a span. How brief it seems on looking back! When I remember the brother who died in yonder pew last Sunday, I can but feel how near heaven is to some among us. We have touched the celestial country; one brother has just leaped on shore. The other day, on a sudden, I saw the white cliffs of Dover. The swift ship had performed the passage so rapidly that the sea had been crossed before I had reckoned on reaching land. There were the cliffs. Just ahead. Brethren, heaven is just ahead!

"Eternal Life Within Present Grasp,"
Metropolitan Tabernacle Pulpit, No. 1946 (1887)

SING TO THE LORD

I will sing of the mercies of the LORD for ever: with my mouth will I make known thy faithfulness to all generations. For I have said, Mercy shall be built up for ever: thy faithfulness shalt thou establish in the very heavens.

PSALM 89:1–2

This psalm is one of the very choicest songs in the night. Midst a stream of troubled thoughts there stands a fair island of rescue and redemption, which supplies standing room for wonder and worship while the music of the words, like the murmuring of a river, sounds sweetly in our ears.

Read the psalm carefully and it will rouse your sympathy, for he who wrote it was bearing bitter reproach and was almost brokenhearted by the grievous calamities of his nation. Yet his faith was strong in the faithfulness of God, and so he sang of the stability of the divine covenant when the outlook of circumstances was dark and cheerless. Nor did he ever sing more sweetly than he sang in that night of his sorrow. Greatly doth it glorify God for us to sing His high praises in storms of adversity and on beds of affliction. It magnifies His mercy if we can bless and adore Him when He takes as well as when

He gives. It is good that out of the very mouth of the burning fiery furnace there should come a yet more burning note of grateful praise.

I am told that there is a great deal of relief to sorrow in complaining; that the utterance of our murmurs may sometimes tend to relieve our pain or sorrow. I suppose it is so. Certainly it is a good thing to weep, for I have heard it from the mouth of many witnesses. Most of us have felt that there are griefs too deep for tears, and that a flood of tears proves that the sorrow has begun to abate. But, methinks, the best relief for sorrow is to sing; this man tried it, at any rate.

Brothers and sisters, I want you at this time to feel the spirit of gratitude within your hearts. What though your mind should be heavy, your countenance sad, and your circumstances gloomy, still let the generous impulse kindle and glow. Oh, come, let us sing unto the Lord.

"Maschil of Ethan,"
Metropolitan Tabernacle Pulpit, No. 1565 (1880)

GOD IS EVERYWHERE

Who knoweth not in all these that the hand of the LORD hath wrought this? In whose hand is the soul of every living thing, and the breath of all mankind.

JOB 12:9–10

There is no event, however base and vile, however grand and good, which is not within the management of the dread Supreme. His dominion hath no limit. He makes the clouds His chariot and yokes the whirlwinds to His car.

Be of good cheer, beloved; in every event you may behold your God. If invasion should ravage this fair island, if tyrants should set their foot on the neck of your liberties, if the streets should run with blood, God were even there supreme; His people still secure. And if it be so that God is in every event, permit me to remind you that God is where there is no event. When there is a lull upon the waters and all is stagnant, when political affairs are quiet, when in the lesser world of your own house and your own soul there is a dead calm, perhaps the woeful prelude of a tempest, God is there.

Great God, Thou standest in the midst of the silent desert, where not even the hum of the bee disturbs the dread solemnity of stillness! Thou art far down in the cleft of the rock where creature could not live! Nay, in the bowels of the solid adamant Thou hast Thy palace, and beneath the surging of the ever-tossing sea Thou hast a tabernacle. In the unknown ravine, the untraversed gorge, the Lord Jehovah hath His dwelling place. He keeps yon rocks from tottering to their fall. He swells those rivers till they roll along.

Let Him but remove His hand, and earth's pillars totter to their fall, creation reels, and the universe expires. As dies the spark struck from the steel, so dies creation if God ceases to be present there. Oh, learn then evermore, that not only in His doings but in His restings, not only in His actings but in His standing still, God is most manifest to you if you will but see Him, if your eyes anointed with heavenly eye salve are but open to behold your Father and your King.

"Everywhere and Yet Forgotten,"
New Park Street Pulpit, No. 326 (1860)

THE OBJECTS OF GOD'S LOVE

But God hath chosen the foolish things of the world to confound the wise; and God hath chosen the weak things of the world to confound the things which are mighty; and base things of the world, and things which are despised. . .that no flesh should glory in his presence.

1 Corinthians 1:27–29

"In the world ye shall have tribulation" is as sure a promise as that other, "In me ye shall have peace." The trials of God's servants are sometimes extremely severe. Not a few are literally as well as spiritually poor. Hunger, privation, and embarrassment haunt their steps. And when you once come to be poor, how often does it happen that you have no helper.

In the summer of prosperity your friends and acquaintances are numerous as the leaves of the forest; but in the winter of your losses and distresses, your friends are few indeed. Your neighbors stand aloof, your old mates desert you; for like the wind, your trials have borne them all away as sere leaves, and you cannot find them. But do not think that the Lord has cast you off, because He is thus chastening you with the rod of men; take it as an exercise of your faith and go to Him.

Did not Jesus lift His eyes to heaven full of gratitude and say, "I thank thee, O Father, Lord of heaven and earth, that thou hast hid these things from the wise and prudent, and hast revealed them unto babes. Even so, Father, for so it seemed good in thy sight"? God hath chosen the poor of this world; He hath chosen the things that are despised and (as the apostle puts it), "Things that are not hath God chosen to bring to nought the things that are, that no flesh should glory in his presence."

When the chariot of the Eternal comes from above, He bids it roll far downward from the skies; He passes by the towers of haughty kings; He leaves the palaces of princes and the halls of senates, and down to the hovels of cottagers the chariot of His grace descends, for there He sees with joy and delight the objects of His everlasting love.

"The Poor Man's Friend,"
Metropolitan Tabernacle Pulpit, No. 1037 (1872)

A STRONG TOWER

The name of the Lord is a strong tower:
the righteous runneth into it, and is safe.

Proverbs 18:10

Troubles, like files, take away our rust; like furnaces, they consume our dross; like winnowing fans, they drive away the chaff. And we should have had but little value, we should have had but little usefulness, if we had not been made to pass through the furnace. But in all our troubles we have found the character of God a comfort.

You have been poor—very poor. I know some of you here have been out of work a long time, and you have wondered where your bread would come from, even for the next meal. Now what has been your comfort? Have you not said, "God is too good to let me starve; He is too bountiful to let me want"? And so, you see, you have found His character to be your strong tower.

Or else you have had losses—many losses—and you have been apt to ask, "How can these things be? How is it I have to work so long and plod so hard, and have to look about me with all my wits to earn but little, and yet when I have made money it melts?" Then we are apt to think that God is unwise to let us toil for naught. But, lo, we run into our strong tower and we feel it cannot be. No, the God who sent this affliction could not have acted in a thoughtless, reckless, wisdomless manner; there must be something here that shall work for my good.

Perhaps your trial has been want, and then you have said, "His name is Jehovah-Jireh, the Lord will provide"; or else you have been banished from friends, perhaps from country, but you have said, "Ah! His name is Jehovah-Shammah, the Lord is there"; or else you have had a disturbance in your family; there has been war within, and war without, but you have run into your strong tower, for you have said, "His name is Jehovah-Shalom, the Lord send peace"; or else many have been your enemies, then His name has been "Jehovah-Nissi, the Lord my banner"; and so He has been a strong tower to you. Defy, then, brethren—defy, in God's strength, tribulations of every sort and size.

"Our Stronghold,"
Metropolitan Tabernacle Pulpit, No. 491 (1862)

YET SHALL I RISE

Rejoice not against me, O mine enemy:
when I fall, I shall arise.

MICAH 7:8

The grounds of a believer's peace are always the same, but a believer's enjoyment of that peace varies very greatly. I always have a right to the divine inheritance, but I do not always enjoy the fruits of that inheritance. Peace may be broken with the Christian, through great trouble, if his faith is not very strong. It need not be so, for some of those who have had the greatest fight of affliction have had the sweetest peace in Christ Jesus.

Peace may be broken through some forms of disease, which prey upon the mind as well as the body; and when the mind grows weak and depressed from what are rather physical causes than spiritual ones, the infirmity of the flesh is apt to crush spiritual peace. Yet it is not always so, for sometimes, when heart and flesh have failed, yet God has been the strength of our heart, as He is our portion forever.

Inward conflict too may disturb our enjoyment of peace. When a man is struggling hard against a sin, when some old habit has to be hanged up before the Lord, when corruption grows exceedingly strong and vigorous, as at seasons it may do, the believer may not enjoy peace as he would wish. And yet I have known warring times when the fight within has not diminished my peace.

"How so?" you may say. I have found peace in the very fact that I was fighting! I have seen clearly that if I were not a child of God, I should not struggle against sin. The very fact that I contend against sin as against my deadliest foe proves that I am not under the dominion of sin; and that fact brings to my soul a measure of peace.

Satan too—oh, it is hard to have peace under his attacks! He has a way of beating his hell-drum at a rate which will let no believer rest. He can inject the most profane thoughts; he can flutter us and worry us by making us think that we are the authors of the thoughts which he fathers upon us—which are his, and not ours. It is a very glorious thing, then, to be able to say, "Rejoice not over me, O mine enemy; though I fall, yet shall I rise again."

"Peace: How Gained, How Broken,"
Metropolitan Tabernacle Pulpit, No. 2112 (1889)

MORE IN GOD TO CHEER YOU

Wilt thou not revive us again:
that thy people may rejoice in thee?

Psalm 85:6

There are many causes for joy to a Christian, but the great wellhead is God Himself. I can rejoice in His people, but then they have their faults. I can rejoice in His Word, but then I sometimes tremble at that Word. I can rejoice in God's works, but then there is a certain terror even about them. But as for God, He Himself is perfect. And whether He is dressed in robes of war or comes to me with words of peace, now that I am reconciled to Him by the death of His Son, He is altogether delightful under any aspect and in any place.

It may seem a very little thing for us thus to delight in God, but it is the greatest thing of all. It is the crown of a revival that God's people should rejoice in Him.

Now, dear hearts, as you come to the communion table, I want you to try to rejoice in God. "But I am mourning about myself," says one. Well, mourn about yourself if you like, but do rejoice in God. "Oh, but I am troubled in my circumstances!" Well, but a child of God should rise above circumstances and rejoice in God. There is more in God to cheer you than in your circumstances to depress you.

Say to all these things, "Good-bye! Good-bye! Go home, for tonight I am just going to rejoice in God to the full." God help you so to do, and if you do, I shall know that the revival has come, and we shall look to see other fruits of it, seeing that this best and sweetest fruit of all is already reached.

"A Prayer for Revival,"
Metropolitan Tabernacle Pulpit, No. 2426 (1887)

HE'S THE GOD OF SMALL THINGS

And God opened her eyes, and she saw a well of water; and she went, and filled the bottle with water, and gave the lad drink.

Genesis 21:19

There was a well of water close to Hagar all the while, though she saw it not. God did not cleave the earth and cause new waters to gush forth, nor was there need. The well was there already, but for all practical purposes it might not have been there, for she could not see it. The water was spent in her bottle, her child was dying with thirst, and she herself was ready to faint—and yet the cool spring was bubbling up hard by the spot. It was needful that she should see the well, quite as needful as that the well should be there, and therefore the Lord in great compassion led her to see it, or as the text puts it, "God opened her eyes."

This was a small matter compared with the creation of a new fountain, but our God does very little things as well as very great things when there is need for them. The same God who divides the Red Sea, and makes the Jordan to be dried up, opens a poor woman's eyes. The same God who came with all his chariots of fire to Paran, and with all His holy ones to Sinai and made the mountain utterly to smoke in His presence, is He of whom we read, "and God opened Hagar's eyes." The infinite Lord is at home in doing little things; He counts the stars, but He also numbers the hairs of our heads.

Remember that the same God who molded the orb on which we dwell also fashions every tiny dewdrop, and He who makes the lightning bolt to fly through the midst of heaven wings every butterfly and guides every minnow in the brooklet. He prepared a great fish to swallow Jonah, but He also prepared a little worm to destroy the gourd. How condescending He is since He carefully attends to minor matters for His children, and not only kills for them the fatted calf, but puts shoes on their feet. The Lord worketh gloriously by agents and events small and despised.

"Eyes Opened,"
Metropolitan Tabernacle Pulpit, No. 1461B (1879)

JESUS WILL NOT LET YOU DROWN

But when he saw the wind boisterous, he was afraid; and beginning to sink, he cried, saying, Lord, save me. And immediately Jesus stretched forth his hand, and caught him, and said unto him, O thou of little faith, wherefore didst thou doubt?

MATTHEW 14:30–31

Here let me now begin to argue with such of you as are the people of God, who are in sore trouble lest Christ should leave you to sink. Let me forbid your fears by a few words of consolation.

You are now in Peter's condition; you are like Peter—*you are Christ's servant*. Christ is a good master. You have never heard that He suffered one of His servants to be drowned when going on His errands. Will He not take care of His own? Shall it be said at last that one of Christ's disciples perished while he was in obedience to Christ? I say He were a bad master if He should send you on an errand that would involve your destruction. Peter, when he was in the water, was where his master had called him to be; and you in your trouble now, are not only Christ's servant, but you are where Christ has chosen to put you.

Your afflictions, remember, come neither from the east nor from the west; neither doth your trouble grow out of the ground. All your suffering is sent upon you by your God. The medicine which you now drink is compounded in heaven. Every grain of this bitterness which now fills your mouth was measured by the heavenly physician. There is not an ounce more trouble in your cup than God chose to put there. Your burden was weighed by God before you were called to bear it. You are where God put you.

Ask yourself this question then: Can it be possible that Christ would put His own servant into a perilous condition and then leave him there? I have heard of fiends in fables tempting men into the sea to drown them; but is Christ a Siren? Will He entice His people onto the rocks? Will He tempt them into a place where He shall destroy them? God forbid. If Christ calls thee into the fire, He will bring thee out of it; and if He bids thee walk the sea, He will enable thee to tread it in safety.

"Mr. Fearing Comforted,"
New Park Street Pulpit, No. 246 (1859)

HOPE OF MORNING

I can do all things through Christ which strengtheneth me.

PHILIPPIANS 4:13

These Philippians had realized that they were in Christ by a real and vital union with Him. They had come to feel not like separated individualities, copying a model, but as members of a body made like to their head. By a living, loving, lasting union they were joined to Christ as their covenant head. They could say, "Who shall separate us from the love of God which is in Christ Jesus our Lord?"

Do you know what it is to feel that the life which is in you is first in Christ, and still flows from Him, even as the life of the branch is mainly in the stem? "I live; yet not I, but Christ liveth in me." This is to be in Christ. Are you in Him in this sense? It is in Him, and in Him only, that spiritual life is to be sustained, even as only from Him can it be received. To be engrafted into Christ is salvation; but to abide in Christ is the full enjoyment of it. True union to Christ is eternal life.

This expression is very short but very full: "In Christ." Does it not mean that we are in Christ as the birds are in the air which buoys them up and enables them to fly? Are we not in Christ as the fish are in the sea? Our Lord has become our element, vital and all surrounding. In Him we live and move and have our being. He is in us, and we are in Him. We are filled with all the fullness of God, because in Christ doth all fulness dwell—and we dwell in Him. Christ to us is all, He is in all, and He is all in all! Jesus to us is everything in everything.

Without Him we can do nothing, and we are nothing. Thus are we emphatically in Him. If you dwell in the secret place of the tabernacles of the Most High, abide under the shadow of the Almighty. Do you sit at His table and eat of His dainties? Then prolong the visit and think not of removal. Has Jesus brought you into His green pastures? Then lie down in them. Go no further, for you will never fare better. Stay with your Lord, however long the night, for only in Him have you hope of morning.

"THE WATCHWORD FOR TODAY: 'STAND FAST,'"
METROPOLITAN TABERNACLE PULPIT, NO. 1959 (1887)

"CHRIST IS GRAND AT EMERGENCIES"

For they considered not the miracle of the loaves.

MARK 6:52

If the disciples had considered the miracle of the loaves they would have observed that Christ is grand at emergencies. When there were five thousand people to be fed, and no towns and villages near enough to supply them with bread so that the people must faint by the way ere they could reach the markets, then Christ was ready, full-handed in time of scarcity, prompt to dispense His liberality, able to meet the emergency so perfectly that the people must have been very thankful that such an emergency had arisen—and no doubt often wished that they could have been in such a strait again if they could have had the Lord near to bring them out of it. Had they considered the miracle of the loaves, the disciples would have known that Christ not only is grand at emergencies, but that He displays His power spontaneously, without need of pressing or even prompting.

Before anybody else had cared for the multitude, He began enquiring about the state of the stores from which the famishing must be fed. He it was who thought of the way of feeding them; it was a design invented and originated by Himself. His followers had looked at their little store of bread and fish and given up the task as hopeless; but Jesus, altogether unembarrassed and in no perplexity, had already considered how He would banquet the thousands and make the fainting sing for joy. The Lord of Hosts needed no entreaty to become the host of hosts of hungry men.

Remembering this, the disciples in their new distress should have said within themselves, "Now will He display His power. We have scarcely need to cry to Him, for before we call He will answer; and while the emergency is yet pressing upon our minds He will hear." But they forgot what He had done on that occasion, and therefore they fell into distrust as to their new trial. Beloved, is not this a very common fault with us? Do we not too oft forget what the Lord has done for us in times past? We sing so rightly—

His love in time past forbids me to think
He'll leave me at last in trouble to sink;
Each sweet Ebenezer I have in review
Confirms His good pleasure to help me quite through.

"The Miracle of the Loaves,"
Metropolitan Tabernacle Pulpit, No. 1218 (1875)

A FULL CUP

My cup runneth over.

Psalm 23:5

There is a special providence in the endowment of life to each individual creature. David did not disdain to trace back the hand of God to the hour of his nativity, and Paul adored the grace of God that separated him from the time that his mother gave him birth. Our gratitude may, in like manner, revert to the days when we hung upon the breast; or in the case of some, you may thank the goodness that supplied the lack of a mother's tender love.

Childhood's early days might then make our thoughts busy and our tongues vocal with praise. But here we are now. We have been preserved, some of us, these thirty or forty years. We might have been cut down and punished in our sin. We might have been swept away to the place where despair makes eternal night. But we have been kept alive in the midst of many accidents. By some marvelous godsend, death has been turned aside just as it seemed, with a straight course, to be posting toward us. When fierce diseases have been waiting round to hurry us to our last home, we have yet escaped. Nor have we existed merely.

God has been pleased to give us food and raiment and a place whereon to lay our weary heads. To many here present He has given all the comforts of this life, till they can say, "My cup runneth over; I have more than heart can wish."

To all here He has given enough, and though you may have passed through many straits, yet your bread has been given you and your water has been sure. Is not this cause for thankfulness?

You cannot think of a shivering beggar tonight in the streets; you cannot think of the hundreds of thousands in this unhappy country—unhappy for that reason—who have no shelter but such as the poorhouse can afford them and no bread but such as is doled out to them as a pauper's meager pittance, without being grateful that you have been hitherto supplied with things convenient for your sustenance. More than that, we have reason tonight to be very grateful for the measure of health which we enjoy.

"Overwhelming Obligations,"
Metropolitan Tabernacle Pulpit, No. 910 (1870)

THE PEACE OF GOD

And let the peace of God rule in your hearts, to the which also ye are called in one body; and be ye thankful.

COLOSSIANS 3:15

If for the present the will of the Lord should send me poverty, obscurity, pain, weariness, reproach, I must be at peace with God about it all. If the Lord says to me, "Go across the sea, and leave all your friends," I must not delay. If He says, "Preach unwelcome truth, which will make you enemies," I must not hesitate. If He says, "Keep the house with rheumatism," I must not come out of doors. If the Lord says, "Lie on thy back and cough," it is not for me to quarrel with Him and say it ought not so to be.

If He denies us that which we think would make us not only more happy but more useful, it is of no use for us to kick against the pricks. The divine appointment will certainly be fulfilled, and the misery to us will be in struggling against the yoke, in endeavoring to have it otherwise than divine love and infinite wisdom have determined it should be. If thou canst not change thy place, change thy mind, till thy mind shall take to thy place and thou shalt love it.

Why, there have been men so helped of God to conquer self that they have hugged their crosses. I think it is Rutherford who somewhere says that he was half afraid lest he should begin to love his cross better than Christ. That is a fear which will seldom need to cross our minds; but, oh, we ought to be perfectly satisfied, perfectly content with that which pleases God! "If this be the Lord's will, it is my will." Such a saying comes from a happy heart; but if God has one will and we have another, it is clear that the peace of God does not yet rule our hearts."

The point with us is to say, "It is all given up. Whatsoever thou willest, Lord, I will; or at least I wish to will. I ask for grace that I may will it, because Thou willest it." This voluntary submission to our Father's appointment is the peace of God.

"That Horrible East Wind!"
Metropolitan Tabernacle Pulpit, No. 1693 (1882)

IN DUE SEASON

And let us not be weary in well doing:
for in due season we shall reap, if we faint not.

GALATIANS 6:9

While the husbandman waits with his eye upward, he waits with his hands at work, engaged in restless toil. He sows, and it is a busy time. When he sees the green blade, what then? He has to work. Those weeds must not be suffered to outgrow the wheat and choke it. Up and down the field the laborer must go, and the husbandman must be at the expense of this; and all along until the wheat is ripened there is sure to be something to do in this field, so his eyes must be keen, his skill must be taxed, and no drudgery must be disdained.

In all labor there is profit, but nothing is gained without pains. We look up to God. He will not accept the look of a sluggard. The eye that looks up to God must be attended with the hand that is ready for work. So if I suffer and expect the blessing for the suffering, I must spend solitary hours in my chamber seeking and searching; to wit, seeking in prayer and searching God's Word for the blessing. If I am a worker, I must look to God for the result; but then I must also use all the means. In fact, the Christian should work as if all depended upon him, and pray as if it all depended upon God. He should be always nothing in his own estimation; yet he should be one of those gloriously active nothings of which God makes great use, for He treats the things that are not as though they were and gets glory out of them.

Yes, the husbandman waits. He cannot push on the months; he cannot hasten the time of the harvest home; but he does not wait in silence, in sluggishness, and negligence. He keeps to his work and waits too. So do you, O Christian men! Wait for the coming of your Lord, but let it be with your lamps trimmed and your lights burning, as good servants attending to the duties of the house, until the master of the house returns to give you the reward.

"A Visit to the Harvest Field,"
Metropolitan Tabernacle Pulpit, No. 1025 (1871)

THE LORD OF PEACE

Now the Lord of peace himself give you peace always by all means. The Lord be with you all.

2 Thessalonians 3:16

O friends, Christ has peace enough and to spare. He is Himself, personally, the deep wellspring of an endless peace—and therefore we can understand why we always find peace in Him. One calm and quiet man has sometimes spread peace through what else would have been terrified company.

One Paul standing in the sinking ship saves all from ruin by the majesty of his immovable courage; and one Christ—such a Christ as ours—in the midst of a church turns a horde of cowards into an army of heroes. His infinite peace breathes peace into our vacillating spirits. We rest because we see how He rests.

Now, as the Master had peace in Himself, He had a strong desire that all His disciples should have peace. I was about to say that it was with our Lord "the ruling passion strong in death." It was strong within Him when He was coming very near His passion and was about to go into Gethsemane and then to Golgotha. Quietly He said, "These things have I spoken unto you, that in me ye might have peace."

Our Lord Jesus Christ delights to see His people firm, calm, happy. I do not think that He is so pleased to see them excited, although we have those around us who seem to think that great grace can only display itself by raving and raging. The religion of the quiet Jesus was never intended to drive us to the verge of insanity. "He shall not strive, nor cry; neither shall any man hear his voice in the streets."

His Holy Spirit is no raven or eagle, but a dove. His holy influences are powerful, and therefore calm. Weakness hurries, rages, shouts; for it has need to do so. Strength moves with its own deliberate serenity, and effects its purpose. To those who think that saints should be maniacs, Jesus says, "Peace! Peace!"

"Sweet Peace for Tried Believers,"
Metropolitan Tabernacle Pulpit, No. 1994 (1887)

PROSPERITY UNDER PERSECUTION

Thou therefore endure hardness,
as a good soldier of Jesus Christ.

2 TIMOTHY 2:3

Dear brother, dear sister, are you passing through great trials? Very well then—to meet them I pray that God's grace may give you greater faith; and if your trials increase more and more, so may your strength increase. You will be acting after God's manner, guided by His wisdom, if you seek to get more faith out of more trial, for that trial does strengthen faith through divine grace. Experience teaches us, and as we make full proof of the faithfulness of God, our courage, once apt to waver, is confirmed. Do pray the Lord that when the trials multiply you may get faith wherewith to meet them; that out of the eater you may get meat, and out of the strong find strength.

So too if you know the truth of God to be at any time assailed, and your own mind is beset with doubt about any doctrine, always ask God so to open that particular truth to your understanding and endear it to your heart, that by the assaults you are enabled to repel, your faith may be the more confirmed.

Oh! There is a light way of holding truth, and there is a tenacious way of grasping it. I have held doctrines, as it were, in my hand like a boy's ball, that might be thrown away. But it is another thing when the King prints the mark of the doctrine right into your very soul, so that you could no more part with it than you could part with life itself. Trials often burn doctrines into us, and heresies and infidelities make the good confession dear in our sight as a prize which we could never part with. Thus opposition to the truth leads to the multiplication of evidences in its support, and the more we are assailed with the arguments of science, falsely so-called, the firmer we adhere to the oracles of God.

Or it may be, dear Christian worker, that of late you have met with a great many discouragements. You seem to have labored in vain, and spent your strength for nought. Ask then, in prayer, and act accordingly, that the more you are defeated the less you may be disposed to yield; but rather that you may be endowed with fresh energy for the service, and strive with increased assurance for the victory.

"PROSPERITY UNDER PERSECUTION,"
METROPOLITAN TABERNACLE PULPIT, NO. 997 (1871)

A WAY TO ESCAPE

There hath no temptation taken you but such as is common to man: but God is faithful, who will not suffer you to be tempted above that ye are able; but will with the temptation also make a way to escape, that ye may be able to bear it.

1 CORINTHIANS 10:13

We do not always dwell upon the mount of transfiguration nor sit at the festival of love in rapturous fellowship, but at times we are thrust into the furnace of soul trouble, and our faces become black as a coal through grief of heart. We find it hard even to retain a spark of faith; we even question whether we are the Lord's, though we resolve to battle on in His name, come what may. Even when by full assurance we can read our title clear we are apt to look forward, and there comes over us the fear that we shall yet fall by the hand of the enemy.

If trials multiply, how will faith be able to stand? When the days of weakness arrive, what shall we do in our old age? Behind all stands the skeleton form of death. What shall we do in the swellings of Jordan? We recollect how we ran with the footmen in our former trials and they wearied us; and we ask ourselves, "How shall we contend with horsemen?" When eternity is close in view and when within a few hours we shall be made to confront the judgment seat, shall we bear it? Will our religion then prove to be a reality, or will our hope dissolve like a dream? Such questions torment our souls.

Now, brothers and sisters, it will not do to try and answer these questions by taking counsel with the flesh. If you consult your own strength, it is clear that you cannot win the life battle. What is your strength but perfect weakness? If you look to your own wisdom, it is evident that you cannot guide your own way across the pathless desert of life. What is your wisdom but the essence of folly?

Come back, then, in childlike confidence to God, and go no more from Him. Come to the very spot where your spiritual life commenced and find strength, wisdom, rest, and all in the living God. No trial shall happen to you but such as is common to man, and when the temptation comes, the way of escape shall come with it.

"ENCOURAGEMENT TO TRUST AND PRAY,"
METROPOLITAN TABERNACLE PULPIT, NO. 1419 (1878)

JESUS PRAYS FOR YOU

Wherefore he is able also to save them to the uttermost that come unto God by him, seeing he ever liveth to make intercession for them.

HEBREWS 7:25

Dear friend, you are troubled this morning. You are cast down, you do not prosper as you could wish in heavenly things; well, but Christ is not troubled, He is not cast down. And the great fight, after all, goes rightly enough; God's great purposes are subserved; Christ is glorified.

Remember that your exalted Savior is exalted to intercede for you. If He hath power, He useth it in prayer for you. Christ has no merit which He does not plead for you. Jesus has received no reward, in consequence of His death, which He will withhold from you. Dear to the Father He is, but He uses that influence on your behalf. Joseph said to the butler, "Speak for me when it shall be well with thee"; but the butler forgot him. It is well with Jesus today and—depend upon it—it is well with you also, for the Well-beloved cannot forget you. And as He always has the Father's ear, He will pray the Father for you, and whatsoever you need shall surely be given you.

Recollect too, that Christ has this power, not only to intercede for you but to prepare a place for you. Christian, if Christ be a king of boundless wealth, yet He disdains not to use the wealth of His royal treasury to furnish that mansion of yours most richly, so as to make it worthy of the giver who shall bestow it upon you. Moreover, Jesus is in glory as your representative. You are virtually in heaven at this very moment in God's esteem. Your representative is there. My head is in heaven; wherefore should I fear? How can God give heaven to the head and hell to the foot? As sure as Christ is there, every one of those who are virtually united to Him shall be there also.

Because He lives, we shall live also; and it is His will that where He is, there should also His people be. Jesus is in heaven full of power—there to intercede, to represent, to prepare; but that far-reaching power darts its rays down to earth. Believe it, Christian, nothing occurs here without the permit or the decree of your Savior, who loved you and gave Himself for you.

"Stephen's Martyrdom,"
Metropolitan Tabernacle Pulpit, No. 740 (1867)

BE SEPARATE

*Wherefore come out from among them,
and be ye separate, saith the Lord, and touch
not the unclean thing; and I will receive you.*

2 CORINTHIANS 6:17

Persecution in the church—even when it does not take the form of burning or imprisonment, but of slander, of cruel mockings, jesting, jeering, and venomous spite—in whatever form it is sent, persecution helps to keep up the separation between the church and the world.

I fear most the rich when they bring gifts. I loathe the world most when it fawns and flatters. When I heard of a lady who had put on Christ by baptism, that the cold shoulder was given her in all the circles in which she moved, did I, think you, feel more disposed to condole or to congratulate? It was said that now she had but few invitations to such places and such society as she had previously frequented, and I rejoiced and thanked God for it. I was glad of it, for I felt she was farther removed from temptation. When I heard of a young man that, after he joined the church, those in his workshop met him at once with loud laughter and reproached him with bitter scorn. I was thankful, because now he could not take up the same position with themselves. He was a marked man; they who knew him discovered that there was such a thing as Christianity, and such a one as an earnest defender of it.

"Come out from among them, and be ye separate, and touch not the unclean thing; and I will receive you, and will be a Father unto you, and ye shall be my sons and daughters." This is a text that needs to be thundered in trumpet tone. What says the great King unto the spouse? "Forget also thine own people, and thy father's house; so shall the King greatly desire thy beauty: for he is thy Lord; and worship thou him." "Be not conformed to this world: but be ye transformed by the renewing of your mind."

Too much laxness, giving way to the world a friendship foil of fascination brings on leanness of spirit, and causes us to be scarcely known as Christians, weakens our testimony, and in every way promotes Satan's ends. But when persecution breaks forth, barriers are set up and distinctive colors are worn, so the two camps are kept in open hostility; and when brought to battle with each other, the church is kept pure with armor bright. Victory waits her march, and her champions win their laurels.

"PROSPERITY UNDER PERSECUTION,"
METROPOLITAN TABERNACLE PULPIT, NO. 997 (1871)

LEAVE IT TO HIM

And I saw heaven opened, and behold a white horse; and he that sat upon him was called Faithful and True, and in righteousness he doth judge and make war.

REVELATION 19:11

One blessing that will always come to God's needy ones is this—Christ will right them, He will judge them with judgment.

Are you harshly spoken of at home? Don't be angry, don't provoke in return, don't answer railing with railing. "He shall judge his poor with righteousness." Leave it to Him. Wait, wait, till the judgment sits, for who are these that they should judge you? Their opinion, though it is bitter as gall to your spirit, does not really affect your character or your destiny. If you are right before the Lord through faith in Christ, they cannot make you wrong by anything they say. God judges and God knows. "He searcheth the heart and tries the reins."

You remember how David, among his brethren, was much despised. He had not the appearance and the carriage that his elder brethren had—and even Samuel, the Lord's prophet, thought the others to be better than David, and said of them, "Surely the Lord hath chosen these." David was therefore despised of his brethren, but what mattered it? The Lord looked not as man looks, for man looked upon the outward appearance, but God looketh at the heart.

Bide your time you that are one of a family and alone. Or, if for Christ's sake you have been despised, have courage tonight and let not your spirit be bowed down. "Rejoice ye in this day and leap for joy, for so persecuted they the prophets that were before you." The King will speedily come, and when He cometh then will this word be verified: "He shall judge his people with righteousness and his poor with judgment." There is one mercy for you—to have your wrongs righted and your character cleared.

God's poor and needy ones, you will perceive, if you turn a little further down, shall be saved from oppression. Christ Himself was oppressed and afflicted, yet He opened not His mouth. His people may expect to be oppressed too; but they have this for their comfort, that Christ will surely deliver them—and He will break their oppressors in pieces.

"The Poor Man's Friend,"
Metropolitan Tabernacle Pulpit, No. 1037 (1872)

GOD IS STILL WITH YOU

The Lord *is nigh unto them that are of a broken heart; and saveth such as be of a contrite spirit.*

Psalm 34:18

The Christian sometimes sinks very deeply in sore trial from without. He loses his property; his children die; his wife is carried to the grave; every earthly prop is cut away. What then? He goes down, down, down; yet still underneath him are the everlasting arms. You cannot sink so deep in distress and affliction, but what the covenant grace of an ever-faithful God will be still lower than you are, even when at your very lowest.

Look at your Savior; you are never so low as He was. Perhaps you cannot pay your rent, and you are to be turned out of that little room; this is falling low indeed. But what did your Savior say—"Foxes have holes, and the birds of the air have nests, but I, the Son of Man, have not where to lay my head." I have supposed you to be in a very sad case but, you see, underneath you there are the sufferings of Christ. Jesus represents the great goodness of God in its communion with your need, and in Him your God puts underneath you His everlasting arms.

Possibly you are sinking very deep down, under trouble

from within. You have felt such vexations of spirit as you never thought you could have known; you have waged such a conflict as you never dreamed of; the fountains of the great deep have been broken up; and, as a deluge, sin threatens to cover your spirit and drown all the life in your heart. Beloved, you cannot even there be brought so low as Christ was, for what did He say—"My God, my God, why hast thou forsaken me?"

God is still with you to be your succor, and if you have lost the light of your Father's countenance, yet you have not lost it to so great an extent as your Savior did; you have not yet sweat "great drops of blood"; you have not yet prayed with strong crying and tears and found that the cup could not be removed altogether. You have not yet descended into the depths, as your Savior did; and so we will take it for granted that underneath you, wherever you may be, there are the everlasting arms.

"PRESENT PRIVILEGE AND FUTURE FAVOR,"
METROPOLITAN TABERNACLE PULPIT, NO. 624 (1865)

EXPECT TROUBLE

This is my comfort in my affliction:
for thy word hath quickened me.

Psalm 119:50

It is almost needless for me to say that, in some respects, the same events happen unto all men alike—in the matter of afflictions it is certainly so. None of us can expect to escape trial. If you are ungodly, "many sorrows shall be to the wicked." If you are godly, "many are the afflictions of the righteous." If you walk in the ways of holiness, you shall find that there are stumbling blocks cast in the way by the enemy. If you walk in the ways of unrighteousness, you shall be taken in snares and held there even unto death. There is no escaping trouble; we are born to it as the sparks fly upward. When we are born the second time, though we inherit innumerable mercies, we are certainly born to another set of troubles, for we enter upon spiritual trials, spiritual conflicts, spiritual pains, and so forth, and thus we get a double set of distresses, as well as twofold mercies.

He who wrote this one hundred and nineteenth Psalm was a good man, but assuredly he was an afflicted man. Many times did David sorrow and sorrow sorely. The man after God's own heart was one who felt God's own hand in chastisement. David was a king, and therefore it would be folly on our part to suppose that men who are wealthier and greater than we are, are more screened from affliction—it is quite the reverse. The higher up the mountain, the more boisterous are the winds. Depend upon it, that the middle state for which Agur prayed, "Give me neither poverty nor riches," is, upon the whole, the best. Greatness, prominence, popularity, nobility, royalty bring no relief from trial, but rather an increase of it. Nobody who consulted his own comfort would enter upon dignities attended with so much labor and sore travail.

Child of God, remember that neither goodness nor greatness can deliver you from affliction. You have to face it, whatever your position in life; therefore face it with dauntless courage and extort victory from it. Yet, even if you do face it, you will not escape it. Even if you cry to God to help you, He will help you through the trouble, but He will probably not turn it aside from you; He will deliver you from evil, but He may yet lead you into trial. He has promised that He will deliver you in six troubles, and that in seven there shall no evil touch you; but He does not promise that either six or seven trials shall be kept off from you. One like unto the Son of God was with the three holy children in the fire, but He was not with them till they were in the fire—at least not visibly, and He was not so with them as either to quench the flame or to prevent their being cast into it.

"My Comfort in Affliction,"
Metropolitan Tabernacle Pulpit, No. 1872 (1881)

TRIM YOUR LAMPS

Then shall the kingdom of heaven be likened unto ten virgins, which took their lamps, and went forth to meet the bridegroom. And five of them were wise, and five were foolish. They that were foolish took their lamps, and took no oil with them: But the wise took oil in their vessels with their lamps. While the bridegroom tarried, they all slumbered and slept. And at midnight there was a cry made, Behold, the bridegroom cometh; go ye out to meet him. Then all those virgins arose, and trimmed their lamps.

MATTHEW 25:1–7

It is of the greatest service to us all to be reminded that our life is but a vapor, which appeareth for a little while and then vanisheth away. Through forgetfulness of this, worldlings live at ease and Christians walk carelessly. Unless we watch for the Lord's coming, worldliness soon eats into our spirit as doth a canker.

If thou hast this world's riches, believer, remember that this is not thy rest, and set not too great a store by its comforts. If, on the other hand, thou dwellest in straitness, and art burdened with poverty, be not too much depressed thereby; for these light afflictions are but for a moment, and are not worthy to be compared with the glory which shall be revealed in us.

Look upon the things that are as though they were not. Remember you are a part of a great procession which is always moving by; others come and go before your own eyes; you see them, and they disappear, and you yourself are moving onward to another and more real world. "'Tis greatly wise to talk with our last hours," to give a rehearsal of our departure, and to be prepared to stand before the great tribunal of the judgment.

Our duty is to trim our lamps against the time when the Bridegroom comes; we are called upon to stand always ready, waiting for the appearing of our Lord and Savior Jesus Christ, or else for the summons which shall tell us that the pitcher is broken at the fountain and the wheel broken at the cistern, that the body must return to the earth as it was, and the spirit unto God who gave it.

"STEPHEN'S DEATH,"
METROPOLITAN TABERNACLE PULPIT, NO. 1175 (1874)

THE BELIEVER IS SAFE

For thou hast been a shelter for me, and a strong tower from the enemy. I will abide in thy tabernacle for ever: I will trust in the covert of thy wings. Selah.

PSALM 61:3–4

The man that is sheltered in his God—a man that dwells in the secret places of the tabernacle of the Most High, who is hidden in his pavilion and is set upon a rock, he is safe; for, first, who can hurt him? The devil? Christ has broken his head. Life? Christ has taken his life up to heaven; for we are dead, and "our life is hid with Christ in God." Death? No; the last enemy that shall be destroyed is death. "O death, where is thy sting? O grave, where is thy victory?" The law? That is satisfied, and it is dead to the believer, and he is not under its curse. Sin? No; that cannot hurt the believer, for Christ has slain it. Christ took the believer's sins upon Himself, and therefore they are not on the believer anymore.

Our names are written on the hands of Jesus; who can erase those everlasting lines? We are jewels in Immanuel's crown. What thievish fingers shall steal away those jewels? We are in Christ. Who shall be able to rend us from His innermost heart? We are members of His body. Who shall mutilate the Savior? "I bare you," saith God, "as on eagles' wings." Who shall smite through the breast of the Eternal One, heaven's great eagle? He must first do it ere he can reach the eaglets, the young sons of God, begotten unto a lively hope. Who can reach us? God interposes; Christ stands in the way; and the Holy Spirit guards us as a garrison.

Shall they kill us? Then we begin to live. Shall they banish us? Then we are but nearer to our home. Shall they strip us? How can they rend away the garment of imputed righteousness? Shall they seize our property? How can they touch our treasure since it is all in heaven? Shall they scourge us? Sweet shall be the smart when Christ is present with us. Shall they cast us into a dungeon? What fetters can bind the man who is free in Christ? The believer is—he must be—safe.

"Our Stronghold,"
Metropolitan Tabernacle Pulpit, No. 491 (1862)

SERVE WHERE YOU ARE

But as God hath distributed to every man,
as the Lord hath called every one, so let him walk.

1 CORINTHIANS 7:17

Every child of God is where God has placed him for some purpose; and the practical use of this point is to lead you to inquire for what practical purpose has God placed each one of you where you now are? You have been wishing for another position where you could do something for Jesus; do not wish anything of the kind, but serve Him where you are.

If you are sitting at the King's gate there is something for you to do there, and if you were on the queen's throne, there would be something for you to do there; do not ask either to be gatekeeper or queen, but whichever you are, serve God therein. Brother, are you rich? God has made you a steward, take care that you are a good steward. Brother, are you poor? God has thrown you into a position where you will be the better able to give a word of sympathy to poor saints. Are you doing your allotted work? Do you live in a godly family? God has a motive for placing you in so happy a position. Are you in an ungodly house? You are a lamp hung up in a dark place;

mind you, shine there. Esther did well, because she acted as an Esther should, and Mordecai did well, because he acted as a Mordecai should.

I like to think, as I look over you all—God has put each one of them in the right place, even as a good captain well arranges the different parts of his army; and though we do not know his plan of battle, it will be seen during the conflict that he has placed each soldier where he should be. Our wisdom is not to desire another place, nor to judge those who are in another position; but each one being redeemed with the precious blood of Jesus should consecrate himself fully to the Lord and say, "Lord, what would Thou have me to do? For here I am, and by Thy grace I am ready to do it." Forget not then the fact that God in His providence places His servants in positions where He can make use of them.

"Providence—As Seen in the Book of Esther,"
Metropolitan Tabernacle Pulpit, No. 1201 (1874)

NOTHING TO FEAR

Then they cry unto the Lord *in their trouble, and he bringeth them out of their distresses. He maketh the storm a calm, so that the waves thereof are still. Then are they glad because they be quiet; so he bringeth them unto their desired haven.*

Psalm 107:28–30

We ought to be a bold race of people. What have we to fear? Another man looks up, and if he sees a lightning flash, he trembles at its mysterious power. We believe it has its predestined path. We may stand and contemplate it; although we would not presumptuously expose ourselves to it, yet can we confide in our God in the midst of the storm.

We are out at sea; the waves are dashing against the ship; she reels to and fro. Other men shake, because they think this is all chance; we, however, see an order in the waves and hear a music in the winds. It is for us to be peaceful and calm. To other men the tempest is a fearful thing; we believe that the tempest is in the hand of God. Why should we shake? Why should we quiver?

In all convulsions of the world, in all temporal distress and danger, it is for us to stand calm and collected, looking boldly on. Our confidence should be very much the same, in comparison with the man who is not a believer in providence, as the confidence of some learned surgeon, who, when he is going through an operation, sees something very marvelous, but yet never shudders at it; while the ignorant peasant, who has never seen anything so wonderful, is alarmed and fearful and even thinks that evil spirits are at work. We are to say—let others say what they please—"I know God is here, and I am His child, and this is all working for my good; therefore will not I fear, though the earth be removed, and though the mountains be carried into the midst of the sea."

There are some of you who are frightened at every little thing. Oh! If you could but believe that God manages all. As a believer in God's providence, you should just stand and say that God has done it, and it is yours to resign all things into His hands.

"Providence," New Park Street Pulpit, No. 187 (1858)

SAFE SHELTER

He shall cover thee with his feathers, and under his wings shalt thou trust: his truth shall be thy shield and buckler.

PSALM 91:4

When the foundations of enterprise are slackened, and gigantic schemes burst like a bubble; when the mill is at rest, and looks like the hulk of a disabled vessel; when the workshops are closed, and the artisans skilled to labor seek a pauper's pittance at the gates of the union; or when the affliction falls upon the fields and the folds, a blight destroying the crops, and rinderpest cutting down the oxen—these are the sorrows of the world, and chosen men of old have trusted in God nor found Him to fail in straits like these.

So said one, "Although the fig tree shall not blossom, neither shall fruit be in the vines; the labor of the olive shall fail, and the fields shall yield no meat; the flock shall be cut off from the fold, and there shall be no herd in the stalls: yet will I rejoice in the LORD, I will joy in the God of my salvation."

Yet more, brethren, who among you need be reminded of the fears that seize the breast when pestilence is spreading through the land, and rumors that it has approached your own doors have reached your ears? Neighbors or kinsfolk are smitten down without warning. With anxious looks and eager enquiries you listen for tidings that 'twere well nigh death to hear. Have you never counted the watches of the night, dreading every sound, and pondering every sensation you felt, as if it were an ominous portent? When the cholera has been raging, or the fever has been making havoc; when science has been baffled to find out the cause or cure of some insidious disease that walketh in darkness and wasteth at noonday; when those who were wont to jeer at religion and laugh at prayer have said, "This is no doubt a visitation of God."

Pluck up courage, and say within yourselves, "Now will I prove that promise true, 'He shall cover thee with his feathers, and under his wings shalt thou trust.'" Blessed be God, the promise before us is available for sunshiny days, yea, for every hour of this mortal life.

"Safe Shelter,"
Metropolitan Tabernacle Pulpit, No. 902 (1869)

PREPARED FOR AFFLICTION

For our light affliction, which is but for a moment, worketh for us a far more exceeding and eternal weight of glory.

2 CORINTHIANS 4:17

You are not screened from any kind of trouble. You are in Christ, and the Savior saves you from your sins, but He has not promised that you shall have no sorrow. He has not promised to screen you from either poverty or toil or sickness or slander or any of the common ills of mankind.

Some of the very best of His beloved have been enriched and indulged by being permitted to undergo much secret discipline of pain and sorrow and want. Your Lord, among the treasures that He gives you, grants a cross. You start back and say, "Not that, Lord"; but He answers, "Yes, this, my child. This and no other." The cross is the best piece of furniture in your house, though you have sometimes wished it was not there. It shall always work your good; it does work it now.

Some of the comforts allotted to you in providence will be questionable in their effect upon you, by reason of your sinfulness and weakness; but the cross which the Lord appoints you has no result but your good. It is a bitter tree, apparently, but it is a healthful medicine. Take it, child of God; plant it and let it grow, and its fruit shall be sweet. We are not guarded from tribulation, but we are promised it, and we are benefited by it.

We are not favored by being promised the admiration of the ungodly. "In the world"—not merely in this present state, but in this ungodly world—we shall have tribulation. When the world pretends to love, understand that it now hates you more cordially than ever and is carefully baiting its trap to catch you and ruin you. Beware of the Judas kiss with which the Christ was betrayed, and with which you will be betrayed unless you are well upon your guard. In the world and from the world ye shall have tribulation. Affliction is not with us always, but it is well to be always prepared for it.

"Sweet Peace for Tried Believers,"
Metropolitan Tabernacle Pulpit, No. 1994 (1887)

GOD KNOWS

My presence shall go with thee, and I will give thee rest.

EXODUS 33:14

The Lord knoweth them that are His; He knows whom He gave to His Son, and He knows that these shall be His jewels forever and ever. Beloved, when you do not know your own mind, God knows His mind. Though you believe not, He abideth faithful; when you are in the gloom, He is light, and in Him is no darkness at all. Your way may be closed, but His way is open. God knows all when you know nothing at all.

When Moses came out of Egypt, he had no plan as to the march of Israel. He knew that he had to lead the children of Israel to the Promised Land, but that was all. He probably hoped to take them by the shortest cut to Palestine at once. Their journey was far otherwise, but it was all prearranged by the divine mind. It was by no error that the tribes were told to turn and encamp before Pi-hahiroth, between Migdol and the sea. The Lord knew that Pharaoh would say, "They are entangled in the land, the wilderness hath shut them in." There was no going back (for the Egyptians were there), and no going forward (for the Red Sea was there); but the Lord had the way mapped out in His own mind.

When our blessed Lord was surrounded by the hungry crowd, He asked His disciples, "How many loaves have ye?" But "Jesus knew what he would do." He had His thoughts, and He knew them. "Known unto God are all his works from the beginning of the world." "Many, O Lord my God, are thy wonderful works which thou hast done, and thy thoughts which are to usward." Thou hast said, "My counsel shall stand, and I will do all my pleasure"; and it is even so.

Brother, you do not know what is to be done, but the Lord knows for you. O body of Christ, let thy head think for thee! O servant of Christ, let thy Master think for thee. "I know," saith God "the thoughts that I think toward you."

"God's Thoughts of Peace, and Our Expected End,"
Metropolitan Tabernacle Pulpit, No. 1965 (1887)

EARTHQUAKE, NOT HEARTQUAKE

God is our refuge and strength, a very present help in trouble. Therefore will not we fear, though the earth be removed, and though the mountains be carried into the midst of the sea; though the waters thereof roar and be troubled, though the mountains shake with the swelling thereof. Selah.

Psalm 46:1–3

God's people have a sure confidence. Other men build as best they may, but true believers rest upon the Rock of ages. Their confidence is altogether beyond themselves. In this song there is nothing about their own virtue, valor, or wisdom. The heathen moralist boasted that if the globe itself should break, his integrity would make him stand fearless amid the wreck. But the believer has a humbler though a truer reliance. Though the earth be removed he is undismayed, and this does not arise from his own personal self-sufficiency, but from God, who is his refuge and strength. He is fearless, not because of his original stoutness of heart and natural firmness of will, but because he has a God to shelter and uphold him. If he does not fear calamity, it is because he fears God and God alone.

Our psalm begins with God, and with God it ends—"The God of Jacob is our refuge."

We may be as timid by nature as the conies, but God is our refuge. We are as weak by nature as bruised reeds, but God is our strength. We never know what strength is till our own weakness drives us to trust omnipotence, never understand how safe our refuge is till all other refuges fail us. When the earth is removed, and the waters of the sea roar and are troubled, being driven both from land and sea, we hide ourselves in God.

You who are strong in yourselves imagine strength where only weakness can be found. You seek the living among the dead, and substantial confidences amid the "vanity of vanities." If we look to ourselves for courage we shall fail in the hour of trial. When the earth is removed, the mightiest men are the first to shudder—the greatest boasters become the worst cowards. For confidence and peace we must say unto the Lord, "All my fresh springs are in you."

"Earthquake, but Not Heartquake,"
Metropolitan Tabernacle Pulpit, No. 1950 (1887)

COURAGE, PILGRIM

Who shall ascend into the hill of the Lord*?*
or who shall stand in his holy place?

Psalm 24:3

Brethren, do you and I think enough of heaven? Do we not think too much of earth? Do we not think too much of the toil, and too little of the time when it shall all be over? A few more days and you and I, believers, shall have done fighting with Satan, have done with temptations, have done with cares, have done with woes. An hour's work and an eternity of rest! One day's toil; and when I shall have accomplished as an hireling my day, then thou comest, O sweet and gentle rest!

"For they rest from their labors, and their works do follow them." Courage, pilgrim, courage! Up that crag, man! Now put hand and knee to it—up!—for when you have climbed a little higher, ay, but a very little, you shall lie down to rest, and then no more fatigue or sorrow. And there too, when we come to the top of the hill of God, we shall be above all the clouds of worldly care and sin and temptation. Oh! How deep is the rest of the people of God above! How calm is their sky!

No vain discourse shall tempt my soul,
Nor trifles vex my ear.

No need to go out to a business which distracts my longing spirit. No need to toil at a labor which puts my soul into an ill state for prayer; no need to mix with worldly minded men who make a jest of my solemnities and would engage my mind with trifles unworthy of notice.

No, above the world, above its distractions and attractions, my soul shall rise when it shall ascend into the hill of God. And, brethren, what a prospect there shall be from the summit! When we shall mount to the hill of God, what sights we shall see! You know from lofty mountains you can look on that side and see the lakes and the rivers; and on this side the green and laughing valleys; and far away, the wild black forest. The view is wide, but what a view is that which we shall have in heaven!

"Climbing the Mountain,"
Metropolitan Tabernacle Pulpit, No. 396 (1861)

EXULTING IN GOD'S MERCY

We will not hide them from their children, shewing to the generation to come the praises of the L*ORD*, *and his strength, and his wonderful works that he hath done.*

PSALM 78:4

Suppose you cannot write and your influence is very narrow, yet still you shall go on singing of God's praise forever and you shall go on teaching generations yet to come. You Sunday school teachers, you shall be Sunday school teachers forever. "Oh," say you, "no, I cannot credit that." Well, but you shall. You know it will always be Sunday when you get to heaven. There will never be any other day there, but one everlasting Sabbath; and through you and by you shall be made known to angels and principalities and powers the manifold wisdom of God.

I teach some of you now, and I often think you could better teach me—some of you old experienced saints. You will teach me by and by. When we are in glory, we shall all of us be able to tell one another something of God's mercy. Your view of it, you know, differs from mine, and mine from my brother's. You, my dear friend, see mercy from one point; and your wife, even though she be one with you, sees it from another point and detects another sparkle of it which your eye has never caught. So shall we barter and exchange our knowledge in heaven and trade together and grow richer in our knowledge of God there.

We will go on exulting in God's mercy so long as we have any being; and that shall be forever and ever. When we have been in heaven millions of years, we shall not want any other subject to speak of but the mercy of our blessed God—and we shall find auditors with charmed ears to sit and listen to the matchless tale, and some that will ask us to tell it yet again.

They will come to heaven, you know, as long as the world lasts, some out of every generation. We shall see them streaming in at the gates more numerously, I hope, as the years roll by, till the Lord comes; and we will continue to tell to fresh comers what the Lord has done for us.

"Maschil of Ethan, a Majestic Song,"
Metropolitan Tabernacle Pulpit, No. 1565 (1880)

THE FURNACE OF AFFLICTION

Behold, I have refined thee, but not with silver; I have chosen thee in the furnace of affliction.

ISAIAH 48:10

You will not find the saints of God where you do not find the furnace burning round about them. I suppose it will be so until the latest age. Until that time shall come when we shall sit under our own vine and our own fig tree, none making us afraid or daring to attempt it, we must still expect to suffer. Were we not slandered, were we not the butt of ridicule, we would not think ourselves the children of God.

We glory that we stand prominent in the day of battle; we thank our enemies for all their shafts, for each one bears upon it proofs of our Father's love. We thank our foemen for every stab, for it only cuts our armor and rattles on our mail, never reaching the heart. We thank them for every slander they have forged and for every lie they have manufactured, for we know in whom we have believed, and know that these things cannot separate us from His love; yea, we take this as a mark of our being called, that we, as the sons of God, can suffer persecution for righteousness' sake.

It is a fact, I say, that you will find religion in the furnace. If I were asked to find religion in London, I protest the last place I should think of going to look for it would be in yon huge structure that exceeds a palace in glory, where you see men decked out in all the toys which the old harlot of Babylon herself once did love. But I should go to a humbler place than that.

I should not go to a place where they had the government to assist them and the great and the noble of the land to back them up; but I should generally go among the poor, among the despised, where the furnace blazed the hottest. There I should expect to find saints—but not among the respectable and fashionable churches of our land. This is a fact then that God's people are often in the furnace.

"God's People in the Furnace,"
New Park Street Pulpit, No. 35 (1855)

THY JUDGMENT IS BETTER

For at the time appointed the end shall be.

DANIEL 8:19

Do not imagine that God has simply out of His own arbitrary will determined this and that. He doeth as He wills, but He always wills to do that which is in conformity with His high and glorious nature. He never wills an unjust thing; He never wills a really unkind thing. All the appointments of His providence, especially toward His people, are ruled in mercy, in tenderness, in love, and in wisdom, and all are conducive to their highest interest and their greatest happiness.

Oh! But this is a blessed truth. Oh! It is sweet to be able to say, "From this day forth, whatever happeneth to me, be it little or be it great, I am content. For this one thing I know, there shall happen nothing but what God permits; I shall be left to no demon's power; I shall not be cast away like an orphan; I shall not be beyond my Father's eye and my Father's hand; all shall come, and last, and end, as shall please Him, and it shall always please Him that everything that comes shall work for my good if I be one of His people. I may not see it at the time, but it will be so whether I see it or not; all shall happen, every event, in its proper place; every pain according to its proper measure; everything that makes me sigh and cry and groan; every loss and every cross; every slander; everything that seems to hinder me or to thwart my wishes—all shall come and be ruled and managed to make the end which God has promised to bring salvation to my soul and glory to Himself."

O beloved, I do not know where those go for comfort who have not accepted this truth—but I do know that after you have done all you can in toiling for your daily bread, or, as in my case, you have done all you can do in the discharge of Christian service, it is a blessed thing in times of serious difficulty and perplexing dilemma to fall right back into the arms of the ever-ruling God and say, "Thou doest all things well; though things go ill according to my judgment, yet Thy judgment is better than mine, and Thou doest all things right, and let Thy name be glorified."

"A Safe Prospective,"
Metropolitan Tabernacle Pulpit, No. 886 (1869)

HIS MERCY ENDURETH

To him who alone doeth great wonders:
for his mercy endureth for ever.

PSALM 136:4

When I reflect that the Holy Ghost has come down from heaven, and that He has never quitted us but abides with His church to carry out the purposes of grace by convincing men of sin and glorifying Christ, I am encouraged to look for great things. The Holy Ghost is not here in vain. He intends to do great things. If the biggest blasphemer out of hell were reported to be saved today, I should not find it difficult to believe the news.

When I see, in addition to the covenant, the Christ, and the Holy Ghost, all the preparations of the Lord's effectual power for the coming of the Lord, for His glorious reign upon the earth and for the eternal glorification of the redeemed, I am assured in my own soul that the Lord is working upon a wonderful scale, whether we see it or not. Between now and the consummation of all things, wonders are to be common. The pathway of grace shall blaze with splendor. I invite you to enlarge your hope concerning Him who alone "doeth great wonders: for his mercy endureth for ever."

Dear friends, we are not left to promises and preparations. Our faith is continually refreshed by new facts. I have the great happiness of frequently seeing very extraordinary instances of God's grace among sinful men. I will not relate even one of them, but my memory is stored with them. Often my eyes are filled with tears when I grip the hand of a convert who but a little while ago was a blasphemer and injurious, a Sabbath breaker, a drunkard, and sunk in every form of uncleanness.

When I see such a man converted, renewed and made holy because the Lord has met with him and revealed Himself to him through the preaching of the Word, my eyes are filled with tears of wondering joy. When I find that such a poor testimony as I am able to bear is made by God's grace effectual to work a total change of nature, I am overwhelmed with wondering and grateful emotions.

"God the Wonder-worker,"
Metropolitan Tabernacle Pulpit, No. 1981 (1887)

CRUCIFIED TO THE WORLD

But God forbid that I should glory, save in the cross of our Lord Jesus Christ, by whom the world is crucified unto me, and I unto the world.

GALATIANS 6:14

Every citizen of heaven must be taught with thorns and briars, as were the men of Succoth. Every child of God must march through the enemies' land, for Christ says, "I pray not that thou shouldst take them out of the world, but that thou shouldst keep them from the evil."

When is a Christian out of danger? Never. If he be prosperous, then he is apt to grow purse-proud or carnally secure; if adversities press upon him, then he is apt to murmur and to grow unbelieving. There are temptations in the high places of the earth, and the valleys are not without them. When the Christian is in honor he is in great peril. Ah! How many have found the high places to be slippery ones! When the believer is in shame and disrepute, he is in danger too, for many professors have found this cross too heavy for their shoulders.

A believer ought to walk through this world expecting to meet with an enemy behind every hedge, reckoning it a wonder if he shall escape for a single day without a bullet from the foe. You are in an enemy's country, and this enemy is on the alert continually; you may sleep, but the world never sleeps; its customs are always seeking to bind you with their chains; its spirit is creeping over you while you are on the exchange or in the market or even in the family; you will find the very atmosphere of this world tends to make you sleep as do others.

You will have much ado while you are in this state of temptation to stand your ground, and unless you watch and pray, the world will be too much for you. O brethren, I would that we knew the world to be more our enemy than we do, for many walk as if they were friends with this world. But such is not the Christian's position; he can say, "The world is crucified unto me, and I unto the world."

"God Is with Us,"
Metropolitan Tabernacle Pulpit, No. 580 (1864)

WEANING OUR THOUGHTS FROM EARTH

For I reckon that the sufferings of this present time are not worthy to be compared with the glory which shall be revealed in us.

ROMANS 8:18

To a Christian man, must not the world bring tribulation and anguish because it is a world which lieth in the wicked one? The Christian is not of the world, even as Christ is not of the world. He is out of his element. He is an alien. He is a pilgrim. Can he expect the comforts of home while he tarries here? It is a world uncongenial to his spiritual nature. There is nothing in it to help him.

This world is a foe to grace, and not a friend to it—and hence the gracious man must have tribulation. If he is to be like his Lord, he certainly will have it; and if he is to be like the Lord's people, he will have it, for they are a line of cross-bearers. There is no exception to this rule if you take the whole of any believer's life, though for a while certain favored men may seem to be the darlings of providence. Job multiplied his riches and dwelt at ease with a hedge about him. He thought, perhaps, that he would have no tribulation to bear; but the flail seemed made of iron when at last it fell. So may the most prosperous have all the greater trial when the day of adversity arrives.

Though there is tribulation in the world, we still get far too fond of the world. We are always trying to pluck handfuls of its flowers, and if its roses had no thorns we should bury ourselves in heaps of them! We should never quit the nest and learn to fly if the Lord did not stir up our nest even as doth the eagle. We should want to tarry here forever and say, "Lo, this is my home," if it were not that an unkind world gives us aliens' treatment and forces us to feel that here we are in exile. Thanks be unto God for the tribulation which weans our thoughts from earth and wins them for heaven.

"Sweet Peace for Tried Believers,"
Metropolitan Tabernacle Pulpit, No. 1994 (1887)

BEWARE OF DARK THOUGHTS

Do thyself no harm.

ACTS 16:28

When a man sees that his confidences are broken up like a potter's vessel till, to use the expressive figure of the prophet, there is not a piece left large enough to take fire from the hearth or to take water out of the pit, then he is apt to exclaim, "Now it is all over with me, and I must needs perish." You loved your wife—she was all the world to you; but, alas, she is dead, and you cry, "Let me die also." You hugged your wealth, it has melted; that speculation has dissolved it and left you a beggar. And now you cry, "What is there worth living for?"

Beware of dark thoughts which may beset you just now. In your worst moment, should Satan whisper in your ear a suggestion concerning rope or knife or poison bowl or sullen stream, flee from it with all your soul. Obey the apostolic word, "Do thyself no harm." Nothing could be worse for thee than to break the law, which saith expressly, "Thou shalt do no murder." Self-destruction, if done by a man in his senses, is a daring defiance of God and the sealing of damnation. This is to leap from measured trouble into infinite woe, the depth of which none can guess. Why shouldst thou do this?

Turn unto thy God; that is a wiser thing for a man to do than to destroy his own life. Yea, there is something braver for a man to do than to rush upon the pikes of the foe because the battle waxeth too hot for him. Go thou to thy great Captain, even to Him whom God hath given to be a witness to the people, a leader and commander to the people, and He will make thee more than a conqueror.

There are brighter days in store for thee yet. Yea, there are days to come which shall never end, of everlasting life and blessedness if thou wilt but now in thy distress cast thyself upon the covenanted mercies of God in Christ Jesus, His Son. It is grand to spring up from despair into the fullness of delight, and many a man hath done this at a bound.

"ENCOURAGEMENT TO TRUST AND PRAY,"
METROPOLITAN TABERNACLE PULPIT, NO. 1419 (1878)

THOU HAST LACKED NOTHING

For the Lord thy God hath blessed thee in all the works of thy hand: he knoweth thy walking through this great wilderness: these forty years the Lord thy God hath been with thee; thou hast lacked nothing.

Deuteronomy 2:7

We have had much cause to bless the Lord for the abundance of His supplies. Note those four words: "Thou hast lacked nothing." Some things which we could have wished for we have not received, and we are glad they were denied us. Children would have too many sweets if they could, and then they would be surfeited or be ill; we have not been pampered with dangerous dainties, but we have received necessaries, and have lacked nothing.

Walking on in the path of providence, trusting in the Lord, what have we lacked? We have known a few pinches, even as the children of Israel lacked water for the moment but very soon were refreshed with water from the rock; we may have wanted bread for an hour as they did when they were wicked enough to say, "Has the Lord brought us out of Egypt that we may die in the wilderness?" but the clouds before long dropped with a mysterious shower of food for them; and ere long providence has supplied us also.

Our times of straitness have been occasions for appeal to the faithful promise, and we have never appealed in vain. "Thou hast lacked nothing." "No good thing will God withhold from them that walk uprightly." Everything that would be, in the fullest sense, a "good thing," God has given us. If it would be a good thing that we should never again be tempted, if it were a good thing that the devil were buried, if it were a good thing for us to go to heaven at once, we should have all these things; but then there are certain far-reaching purposes to be answered, and to reach them the Lord makes even evils work for the highest good in the ultimate issues of His grand designs.

We ought to magnify the Lord that we have lacked nothing. Praise Him, all ye saints! "Bless the Lord, O my soul, and all that is within me, bless his holy name."

"Forty Years,"
Metropolitan Tabernacle Pulpit, No. 1179 (1874)

PROVIDENCE ORDERS ALL THINGS WISELY

And we know that all things work together for good to them that love God, to them who are the called according to his purpose.

Romans 8:28

None of us have our eyes thoroughly opened yet; we have hitherto been traveling through life as men who journey in a mist. Even the things which have come close to us, and have most affected us, have been hidden, as it were, in that which is not light, but darkness visible. And now, if we could look back upon the whole length of life—forty or fifty or sixty or seventy years—with our eyes opened, how singular it would look!

Why was the favorite son taken away just when all our hopes were to have been fulfilled in him? Why was the husband struck down when the little children were so dependent? Why was the wife removed when a mother's care was most needed? Why fell that daughter sick so suddenly? Why were we ourselves balked in the moment of success?

If our eyes could be opened so that we could see what would have been if things had gone differently, we should all of us thank God that our lives were ordered as they have been. Have you never heard of one who was grievously lamenting the death of his favorite son, and falling asleep dreamed that he saw his boy alive again and that he beheld the life which that son would have led? It was such a life that he wept in his dream, and waking, he blessed God that his son could never act according to what he had seen in vision. It was better that he should be dead.

Repine no more, my sorrowing friend, for that which you would have kept in your bosom might have turned into a viper, that which you thought a treasure might have burned in your heart like coals of fire. Providence has ordered all things wisely, and if our eyes were opened we should bow in adoring reverence and magnify the God who hath done all things well. Our vision will be strengthened one day, so that we shall see the end from the beginning, and then we shall understand that the Lord maketh all things work together for good to them that love Him.

"Eyes Opened,"
Metropolitan Tabernacle Pulpit, No. 1461B (1879)

SAFE AT HOME

The eternal God is thy refuge, and underneath are the everlasting arms: and he shall thrust out the enemy from before thee; and shall say, Destroy them.

DEUTERONOMY 33:27

The eternal God is our mansion, our dwelling, our abiding place. The children of Israel had no other; and therefore if God were not their dwelling place, they were houseless. Pilgrims of the weary foot, they found no city to dwell in; at eventide they pitched their tents, but they struck them again in the morning; the trumpet sounded and they were up and away; if they were in a comfortable valley for one day, yet that relentless trumpet bade them resume their wearisome march through the wilderness in the morning; and perhaps they thought they lingered the longest where an encampment was least desirable.

Nevertheless they always had a dwelling place in their God. If I might use such a description without seeming to be fanciful, I would say that the great cloudy canopy which covered them all day long from the heat of the sun was their roof-tree, and that the blazing pillar which protected them by night was their family fireside. God Himself dwelt in the very midst of them in the bright shining light, the Shekinah, within the holy place, and up from the very spot there rose the great pillar which was cloud by day and fire by night; and so, within the compass of God's protecting presence, they found a perpetual abode.

So Moses sings, "Lord, thou hast been our dwelling place in all generations." Wherever they were, if they were but under the shadow of that cloud they were quite at home; and whenever they got within the radius of the bright pillar of fire, they felt that they were not away from the family circle. At home one feels safe.

An Englishman's house is his castle; who shall intrude upon him there? When the bolt is drawn, when the curtains are closed, when the family gathers round the fireside, then we have shut the world out and all our enemies' babbling tongues, and we dwell in quiet. So, when we get to our God, not bolts of brass nor gates of iron could guard God's people so well as that wall of fire which Jehovah is to all His chosen.

"Present Privilege and Future Favor,"
Metropolitan Tabernacle Pulpit, No. 624 (1865)

GOD'S THOUGHTS TOWARD YOU

For I know the thoughts that I think toward you, saith the L*ORD*, *thoughts of peace, and not of evil, to give you an expected end.*

JEREMIAH 29:11

The Lord not only thinks *of* you, but *toward* you. His thoughts are all drifting your way. This is the way the south wind of His thoughts of peace is moving—it is toward you. The Lord never forgets His own, for He has graven them upon the palms of His hands. Never at any moment does Jehovah turn His thoughts from His beloved, even though He has the whole universe to rule. He saith of His church, "I the Lord do keep it; I will water it every moment: Lest any hurt it, I will keep it night and day." This truth, although it is easily spoken, is not readily comprehended in the fullness of its joy; nor is it always believed as it should be. These people in captivity were likely to fear that their God had forgotten them; hence the Lord repeats His words in this place and speaks of thoughts and thinking three times. His words are so repeated as to seem almost redundant, out of a desire to make His people feel absolutely sure that not only did He *act* towards them but that he still *thought* towards them.

To the banished this would be a grand consolation. The Lord thought of them when they walked the strange streets of "the golden city" and heard a language which they understood not. He thought of them when they were buffeted as aliens by those who marched in the proudest pomp and danced in cruel derision to the sound of their viols. The Lord thought of His exiles when their sole solace was solitude by the brink of the Babylonian canals, where among the willows they remembered Zion.

All that the Lord was doing toward them was done thoughtfully. His thoughts of peace and not of evil toward them had suggested their captivity and the continuance of it for seventy years. If any of you are in trouble and sorrow today, do not doubt that this is sent you according to the thoughtful purpose of the Lord. It is in this fixed intent and thoughtfulness that the real character of an action lies.

"God's Thoughts of Peace, and Our Expected End,"
Metropolitan Tabernacle Pulpit, No. 1965 (1887)

REIGNING WITH CHRIST

If we suffer, we shall also reign with him:
if we deny him, he also will deny us.

2 Timothy 2:12

We have not now to rot in prisons, to wander about in sheepskins and goatskins, to be stoned, or to be sawn in sunder, though we ought to be ready to bear all this if God wills it. The days of Nebuchadnezzar's furnace are past, but the fire is still upon earth. Some suffer in their estates. I believe that to many Christians it is rather a gain than a loss, so far as pecuniary matters go, to be believers in Christ; but I meet with many cases—cases which I know to be genuine, where persons have had to suffer severely for conscience' sake.

There are those present who were once in very comfortable circumstances, but they lived in a neighborhood where the chief of the business was done on a Sunday; when grace shut up their shop, trade left them, and I know some of them are working very hard for their bread, though once they earned abundance without any great toil; they do it cheerfully for Christ's sake, but the struggle is a hard one. I know other persons who were employed as servants in lucrative positions involving sin, but upon their becoming Christians they were obliged to resign their former post and are not at the present moment in anything like such apparent prosperity as they were.

Brethren, ye may possess your souls in patience and expect as a reward of grace that you shall reign with Jesus your beloved. Who can waste his pity over the small griefs of faint hearts, when cold and hunger and poverty are cheerfully endured by the true and brave?

We who live in more enlightened society little know the terrorism exercised in some of the rural districts over poor men and women who endeavor conscientiously to carry out their convictions and walk with Christ. True Christians of all denominations love each other and hate persecution, but nominal Christians and ungodly men would make our land as hot as in the days of Mary, if they dared. To all saints who are oppressed, this sweet sentence is directed—"If we suffer, we shall also reign with him."

"SUFFERING AND REIGNING WITH JESUS,"
METROPOLITAN TABERNACLE PULPIT, NO. 547 (1864)

TIMES OF REFRESHING

The Lord hath done great things for us; whereof we are glad.

Psalm 126:3

Faith is so much attacked, especially in this evil day, that it is like a candle kept alight in a cyclone. Yet you have not drawn back unto perdition! Still, though faint, you are pursuing. Truly if you had been mindful of the country from which you came out, you have had many opportunities to return.

Satan's chariots and his horses have waited upon you with many invitations to ride back into the land of your former slavery if you had a mind to go. Alas! The evil heart of unbelief has lusted for the leeks and garlic and onions many a time. Kept alive with death so near, you are a standing wonder to your own self. What great things the Lord has done for you! How He has led you, instructed you, helped you, comforted you! All these as I mention them will wake up many admiring memories and cause you to cry, "The Lord hath done great things for us; whereof we are glad."

To me, also, it is a great wonder that God should use any of us; we seem so unfit for His holy purposes. Can He write with such a pen as I am upon the fleshy tablets of men's hearts? What! Can He paint a fair picture of holiness in the characters of my hearers with so poor a brush as I am? Then indeed He doeth great wonders. That which God does by our instrumentality at any time—if indeed it be for His glory—should fill us with astonishment. When Saul, who formerly persecuted the saints, saw saints made under his ministry, he was drawn out in wondering adoration as he wrote, "Unto me, who am less than the least of all saints, is this grace given."

The Lord God does wonders still by maintaining His church and the cause of truth in the midst of the world. Read through history and you meet with periods when the light seemed quenched; but then suddenly it burned up with superior luster. Remember the Reformation, and the revival of the last century. When spiritual life seemed almost extinct, there came times of refreshing from the presence of the Lord. It will be the same at this dark hour.

"God the Wonder-worker,"
Metropolitan Tabernacle Pulpit, No. 1981 (1887)

CHRIST CAN CONSOLE YOU

For I know that my redeemer liveth, and that he shall stand at the latter day upon the earth: And though after my skin worms destroy this body, yet in my flesh shall I see God.

Job 19:25–26

Come, my poor heart, lift up thyself now from the dunghill; shake thyself from the dust; ungird thy sackcloth and put on thy beautiful garments. He is our advocate today, our eloquent and earnest pleader, and he prevails with God.

The Father smiles—He smiles on Christ; He smiles on us in answer to Jesus Christ's intercession. Is He not here also the consolation of Israel?

I only remark once more that He who has gone up into heaven shall so come in like manner as He was seen to go up into heaven. He ascended in clouds; "Behold he cometh with clouds." He went up on high with sound of trumpet and with shout of angels. Behold He cometh! The silver trumpet shall soon sound. 'Tis midnight; the hours are rolling wearily along; the virgins wise and foolish are all asleep. But the cry shall soon be heard: "Behold the bridegroom cometh, go ye forth to meet him."

That same Jesus who was crucified shall come in glory. The hand that was pierced shall grasp the scepter. Beneath His arm He shall gather up all the scepters of all kings; monarchies shall be the sheaves, and He shall be the kingly reaper. On His head there shall be the many crowns of universal undisputed dominion. "He shall stand in the latter day upon the earth." His feet shall tread on the Mount of Olivet, and His people shall be gathered in the valley of Jehoshaphat.

Lo, the world's great battle is almost begun; the trumpet sounds the beginning of the battle of Armageddon. To the fight, ye warriors of Christ, to the fight; for it is your last conflict, and over the bodies of your foes ye shall rush to meet your Lord—He fighting on the one side by His coming, you on the other side by drawing near to Him. You shall meet Him in the solemn hour of victory. Then shall you know to the full how Christ can console you for all your sorrows, all your shame, and all your neglect which you have received from the hand of men.

"CONSOLATION IN CHRIST,"
METROPOLITAN TABERNACLE PULPIT, NO. 348 (1860)

STAND FAST

Therefore, my brethren dearly beloved and longed for, my joy and crown, so stand fast in the Lord.

PHILIPPIANS 4:1

Since the Lord has risen and will surely come a second time and will raise the bodies of His people at His coming, there is something to wait for, and a grand reason for steadfastness while thus waiting. We are looking for the coming of our Lord and Savior Jesus Christ from heaven, and that He shall "fashion anew the body of our humiliation, that it may be conformed to the body of His glory." Therefore let us stand fast in the position which will secure us this honor. Let us keep our posts until the coming of the great Captain shall release the sentinels.

The glorious resurrection will abundantly repay us for all the toil and travail we may have to undergo in the battle for the Lord. The glory to be revealed even now casts a light upon our path and causes sunshine within our hearts. The hope of this happiness makes us even now strong in the Lord and in the power of His might.

Paul was deeply anxious that those in whom he had been the means of kindling the heavenly hope might be preserved faithful until the coming of Christ. He trembled lest any of them should seem to draw back and prove traitors to their Lord. He dreaded lest he should lose what he hoped he had gained, by their turning aside from the faith. Hence he beseeches them to "stand fast."

Paul has fought bravely; and in the case of the Philippian converts, he believes that he has secured the victory, and he fears lest it should yet be lost. He reminds me of the death of that British hero, Wolfe, who on the heights of Quebec received a mortal wound. It was just at the moment when the enemy fled, and when he knew that they were running, a smile was on his face and he cried, "Hold me up. Let not my brave soldiers see me drop. The day is ours. Oh, do keep it!"

O my beloved hearers, I believe that many of you are "in the Lord," but I entreat you to "stand fast in the Lord."

"THE WATCHWORD FOR TODAY: 'STAND FAST,'"
METROPOLITAN TABERNACLE PULPIT, NO. 1959 (1887)

THE TRIAL OF YOUR FAITH

That the trial of your faith, being much more precious than of gold that perisheth, though it be tried with fire, might be found unto praise and honuor and glory at the appearing of Jesus Christ.

1 Peter 1:7

It is the honor of faith to be tried. Shall any man say, "I have faith, but I have never had to believe under difficulties"? Who knows whether thou hast any faith? Shall a man say, "I have great faith in God, but I have never had to use it in anything more than the ordinary affairs of life, where I could probably have done without it as well as with it"?

Is this to the honor and praise of thy faith? Dost thou think that such a faith as this will bring any great glory to God—or bring to thee any great reward? If so, thou art mightily mistaken. He that has tested God, and whom God has tested, is the man that shall have it said of him, "Well done, thou good and faithful servant."

If God, then, has given to any one of us a faith which is honorable and precious, it has full surely been submitted to its own due measure of trial; and if it is to be still more precious, it has yet more trials to endure.

The trial of your faith is sent to prove its sincerity. If it will not stand trial, what is the good of it? That gold which dissolves in the furnace and disappears amid the flame is not the gold which shall be current with the merchant; and that faith of thine, which is no sooner tried than straightway it evaporates—art thou not well rid of it? Of what use would it be to thee in the hour of death and in the day of judgment? No, thou canst not be sure that thy faith is true faith till it is tried faith. Thou canst not be certain that it is worth having till it has been fitly tested and brought to the touchstone of trial.

It must also be tested to prove its strength. We sometimes fancy that we have strong faith when, indeed, our faith is very weak; and how are we to know whether it be weak or strong till it be tried? And besides that, dear friends, the trial of our faith is necessary to remove its dross.

"The Trial of Your Faith,"
Metropolitan Tabernacle Pulpit, No. 2055 (1888)

LET NOT YOUR HEART BE TROUBLED

Let not your heart be troubled:
ye believe in God, believe also in me.

JOHN 14:1

There is no need to say, "Let not your heart be troubled," when you are not in affliction. When all things go well with you, you will need another caution: "Let not your heart be exalted above measure: If riches increase, set not your heart upon them."

The word, "Let not your heart be troubled," is timely and it is wise. A few minutes' thought will lead you to see it. It is the easiest thing in the world in times of difficulty to let the heart be troubled. It is very natural to us to give up and drift with the stream, to feel that it is of no use "taking arms against" such "a sea of trouble," but that it is better to lie passive and to say, "If one must be ruined, so let it be."

Despairing idleness is easy enough, especially to evil, rebellious spirits who are willing enough to get into further mischief that they may have more with which to blame God the more, against whose providence they have quarreled. Our Lord will not have us be so rebellious.

He bids us pluck up heart and be of good courage in the worst possible condition; and here is the wisdom of His advice—namely, that a troubled heart will not help us in our difficulties or out of them. It has never been perceived in time of drought that lamentations have brought showers of rain, or that in seasons of frost, doubts, fears, and discouragements have produced a thaw.

We have never heard of a man whose business was declining, who managed to multiply the number of his customers by unbelief in God. I do not remember reading of a person whose wife or child was sick, who discovered any miraculous healing power in rebellion against the Most High. It is a dark night, but the darkness of your heart will not light a candle for you. It is a terrible tempest, but to quench the fires of comfort and open the doors to admit the howling winds into the chambers of your spirit will not stay the storm.

"Let Not Your Hearts Be Troubled,"
Metropolitan Tabernacle Pulpit, No. 730 (1867)

REJOICE IN THE LORD

Although the fig tree shall not blossom, neither shall fruit be in the vines; the labour of the olive shall fail, and the fields shall yield no meat; the flock shall be cut off from the fold, and there shall be no herd in the stalls: Yet I will rejoice in the Lord, *I will joy in the God of my salvation.*

Habakkuk 3:17–18

I am not a little ashamed of myself that I do not live more on high, for I know when we get depressed in spirits and downcast and doubting, we say many unbelieving and God-dishonoring words. It is all wrong. We ought not to stay here in these marshes of fleshly doubts. We ought never to doubt our God. Let the heathen doubt his god, for well he may, but our God made the heavens. What a happy people we ought to be!

When we are not, we are not true to our principles. There are ten thousand arguments in scripture for happiness in the Christian; but I do not know that there is one logical argument for misery. Those people who draw their faces down and, like the hypocrites, pretend to be of a sad countenance, these, I say, cry, "Lord, what a wretched land is this, that yields us no supplies." I should think they do not belong to the children of Israel; for the children of Israel find in the wilderness a rock following them with its streams of water, and manna dropping every day, and when they want them there are the quails; and so the wretched land is filled with good supplies.

Let us rather rejoice in our God. I should not like to have a serving man who always went about with a dreary countenance because do you know people would say, "What a bad master that man has." And when we see Christians looking so sad, we are apt to think they cannot have a good God to trust to.

Come, beloved, let us change our notes, for we have a strong tower and are safe. Let us take a walk upon the ramparts—I do not see any reason for always being down in the dungeon; let us go up to the very top of the ramparts, where the banner waves in the fresh air, and let us sound the clarion of defiance to our foes again, and let it ring across the plain.

"Our Stronghold,"
Metropolitan Tabernacle Pulpit, No. 491 (1862)

JESUS LOVES HIS OWN

Now before the feast of the passover, when Jesus knew that his hour was come that he should depart out of this world unto the Father, having loved his own which were in the world, he loved them unto the end.

JOHN 13:1

Jesus loves His own which are in the world. He sees your imperfection, He knows what you have to struggle with, He understands well enough the uprisings of your nature, and He loves you notwithstanding all.

"Ah!" says another, "I have come hither today, burdened with a very heavy trouble. The partner of my life is sick at home and near to death." "Alas!" cries another, "my dear child is dying, and I found it hard to tear myself away from the bedside." "Worse still," moans another, "I have a living cross to carry; one of my sons is breaking my heart." "Ah!" exclaims a fourth, "I have a bill to meet tomorrow, and I do not know how it will be done. I fear I shall be ruined."

All these things go to show that we are yet in the world of sorrow. As the sparks fly upward, so were we born to trouble—why do we count it a strange thing? But Jesus loves

His own which are in this dolorous world. This is the balm of our griefs, and I call upon you to hold to it, and not let the devil delude you into the idea that the Lord does not love you because affliction happens to you as it does to other men. Of course it must so happen so long as you are in the world. How can you expect exemption?

Would you have a glass case made for you to keep you snug away from all the frosts and winds of this world? Would you have your heavenly Father indulge you with all the sweet things of this life and spoil you for the life to come? Would you strike the root in this world and never be transplanted to the heavenly Eden? Do you wish to have your rest and portion in this life?

Oh! No, you could not wish for that. Well, then, take what God sends to you; receive evil as well as good from Jehovah's hand, as Job aforetime did; but never let it be the thought of your heart that Jesus does not love you.

"The Faithfulness of Jesus,"
Metropolitan Tabernacle Pulpit, No. 810 (1868)

THE LORD'S COMPASSION

They that were scattered abroad went every where preaching the word.

ACTS 8:4

God grants protection to the persecuted and provides an escape from the most perilous exposure. Full often the darkest conspiracy is brought to the direst confusion. No sooner does Christ gather a church in any place, be it a renowned empire or a paltry village, than opposition is stirred up. "If ye were of the world, the world would love his own: but because ye are not of the world, but I have chosen you out of the world, therefore the world hateth you." "I will put enmity between thee and the woman, and between thy seed and her seed," is the first check for the serpent's wiles, the first ray of hope for his helpless victims; and the prediction will continue to be fulfilled till at last, according to the word of the Lord, the tares are bound in bundles to burn them, and the wheat is gathered into His garner.

Whenever there has been a great persecution raised against the Christian church, God has overruled it, as He did in the case of Pharaoh's oppression of the Israelites, by making the aggrieved community more largely to increase. The early persecutions in Judea promoted the spread of the gospel; hence, when after the death of Stephen the disciples were all scattered abroad throughout the regions of Judea and Samaria, except the apostles, the result is thus given: "Therefore they that were scattered abroad went everywhere preaching the word."

So too, when Herod stretched forth his hands to vex certain of the church and killed James, the brother of John, with the sword, what came of it? Why, Luke tells us in almost the same words that Moses had used, "The word of God grew and multiplied."

You shall find in any individual church that wherever evil men have conspired together and a storm of opposition has burst forth against the saints, the heart of the Lord has been moved with compassion, and the hand of the Lord has been raised to succor, till we have come to look upon opposition as an omen of good, and persecution for righteousness' sake as a tearful seed-time, quickly to be followed by a harvest of joy.

"Prosperity Under Persecution,"
Metropolitan Tabernacle Pulpit, No. 997 (1871)

DIVINE PROTECTION

But now thus saith the Lord that created thee, O Jacob, and he that formed thee, O Israel, Fear not: for I have redeemed thee, I have called thee by thy name; thou art mine. When thou passest through the waters, I will be with thee; and through the rivers, they shall not overflow thee: when thou walkest through the fire, thou shalt not be burned; neither shall the flame kindle upon thee.

Isaiah 43:1–2

When you leave your house tomorrow morning, you will little know what peril may befall you during the day. "At least," said an old divine, who was accustomed to spend the most part of his time in his study, "at least the studious man is safe from the accidents which shorten the lives of others." So he vainly thought.

The very day after he had used the expression, a stack of chimneys fell through his study; and had he happened to have been sitting where he customarily did, he must have been crushed to pieces. There are dangers everywhere, and the guardian care of God can never be safely dispensed with.

If we walk aright, we shall never venture upon a single

day without first seeking divine protection. How many who have escaped out of terrible storms have nevertheless died in a calm! Where some have passed through battles without a scar, they have afterwards been killed by an accident so slight that they would utterly have despised a precaution to avoid it.

You always need divine protection; and, believer in Christ, you shall always have it, for "he shall cover thee with his feathers, and under his wings shalt thou trust." This is for you tonight when you strip off your garments and lay your weary frame upon your bed; then you may say, "Now, Lord, cover me with Thy feathers." And it is for you tomorrow, when you are going out to your daily labor, not knowing what may befall you; you can use the same petition: "This day, O God, grant that under Thy wings I may trust."

"Sufficient unto the day is the evil thereof." We ought never to sit down and begin fretting ourselves about what may happen, because the ill we dread may never come to pass.

"Safe Shelter,"
Metropolitan Tabernacle Pulpit, No. 902 (1869)

FERTILE HARVESTS OF JOY

Whether Paul, or Apollos, or Cephas, or the world, or life, or death, or things present, or things to come; all are your's.

1 CORINTHIANS 3:22

Changes in circumstances may arise, poverty may supplant wealth, and slander injure fame; where barns were filled to bursting, there may arise a famine; and those whose broad acres could scarce be traversed in a day may come to a scanty plot of ground, or none at all. But if that do not happen to thee, yet at any rate, thy friends must die if thou do not. Those who in thy younger days were thy familiar acquaintances and companions must pass away, and if thou survivest, thou shalt gradually find thyself, like a lone tree of the forest, when the woodman hath exercised his craft, month after month.

During the lapse of years thy children one by one may die; thy spouse so dear to thy soul may be taken from thee; brethren and sisters may also leave the vale of tears. It must be so. Canst thou hope that the arrows of death will forever turn aside from thy family?

We must expect, sooner or later, that infirmities of body will set in. To some they come, alas! too soon; to all they must come in their time. The windows little by little are darkened, the pillars of the house do tremble, the grinders fail because they are few, and the strong man findeth the grasshopper to be a burden. These things must come; to all men are such trials measured out.

Alas! Our fears find it an easy task to paint a very terrible picture out of these gloomy materials. The pains and groans of our dying strife affright us; the giants, the hills of difficulty and the valleys of humiliation, alarm us; we picture the path of the heavenly pilgrimage as a valley of the shadow of death, throughout full of confusion, dark with adversities, beset with snares, watched over by dragons, and blocked up by Apollyons. There is not in the whole area of our future life a single plot of stony ground which shall not yield us fertile harvests of joy. As Midas of old touched even the most valueless objects and turned them into gold, so does the hand of divine love transmute every trial and affliction into everlasting joy for His people.

"Things to Come,"
Metropolitan Tabernacle Pulpit, No. 875 (1869)

IN TIMES OF TROUBLE

The Lord *is good, a strong hold in the day of trouble; and he knoweth them that trust in him.*

Nahum 1:7

Troubles of every sort and size come upon us, we are vexed with every form of calamity; and yet all the time we are serenely quiet and perfectly happy.

I should think that an eagle aloft there, when he sees the sportsman coming with his gun, however far the bullet may carry, if he knows himself to be quite out of range, would poise himself upon the wing and look down upon the sportsman with a merry heart. Let him send his bullet up into the air as far as it can rise, but the eagle is high above it all; and God gives His children, at times, such mounting faith that they rise up as upon the wings of eagles, and the bullets of trouble cannot reach halfway to them. There, in the clear blue heaven of fellowship with God, they look down on the tops of the clouds and defy all the assaults of man. Happy are they who have thus become God's hidden ones.

There are green meadows, there are still waters; but I believe they are mostly to be found in the places where trials most abound; there, consolations are most plentiful. I hardly think that a man knows the deeps of the serenity of God unless he has been greatly tried. There are wonderful sights that none shall see but those who are hidden away by the Lord in the time of storm and trouble.

Oh, the strife of tongues, the endless babbling of slander! What a blessing not to hear it—or to hear it as a deaf man that heareth not. Oh, the noise of misrepresentation! Oh, the wave upon wave of actual trouble that may come to you in business or in the domestic circle! What joy it is to be just kept out of it all; like Noah in the ark, all the world drowned, but you shut up in safety! And remember that the deeper the floods became, the higher Noah rose toward heaven; so shall it be with you. The more of trial you have to endure, the more of communion you shall have to enjoy. This is the happy, happy case of a tried child of God.

"God's Hidden Ones,"
Metropolitan Tabernacle Pulpit, No. 2367 (1888)

MORE THAN A MATCH

My soul is weary of my life; I will leave my complaint upon myself; I will speak in the bitterness of my soul. I will say unto God, Do not condemn me; shew me wherefore thou contendest with me.

Job 10:1–2

God delighteth in His saints; and when a man delights in his child, if it be a child noted for its brightness of intellect, he delights to see it put through hard questions because he knows that it will be able to answer them all. So God glories in His children. He loves to hear them tried, that the whole world may see that there is none like them on the face of the earth; and even Satan may be compelled, before he can find an accusation against them, to resort to his inexhaustible fund of lies.

Sometimes God on purpose puts His children in the midst of this world's trials. On the right, left, before, behind, they are surrounded. Within and without the battle rages. But there stands the child of God—calm amidst the bewildering cry, confident of victory. And then the Lord pointeth joyously to His saint and He saith, "See, Satan, he is more than a match for thee. Weak though he is, yet through My power, he all things can perform." And sometimes God permits Satan himself to come against one of His children; and the black fiend of hell in dragon's wings meets a poor Christian just when he is faint and weary from stumblings in the valley of humiliation.

The fight is long and terrible; and well it may be, for it is *a worm* combating with *the dragon*. But see what that worm can do. It is trodden underfoot and yet it destroys the heel that treads upon it. When the Christian is cast down he utters a cry, "Rejoice not over me, O mine enemy, for though I fall yet shall I rise again." And so God pointeth to His child and says, "See there! See what I can do. I can make flesh and blood more mighty than the most cunning spirit; I can make poor feeble, foolish man more than a match for all the craft and might of Satan."

"THE SWEET USES OF ADVERSITY,"
NEW PARK STREET PULPIT, NO. 283 (1859)